THE BERLIN COOKBOOK

Berlinica

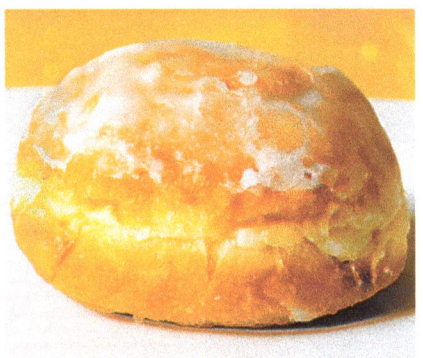

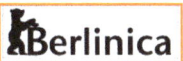

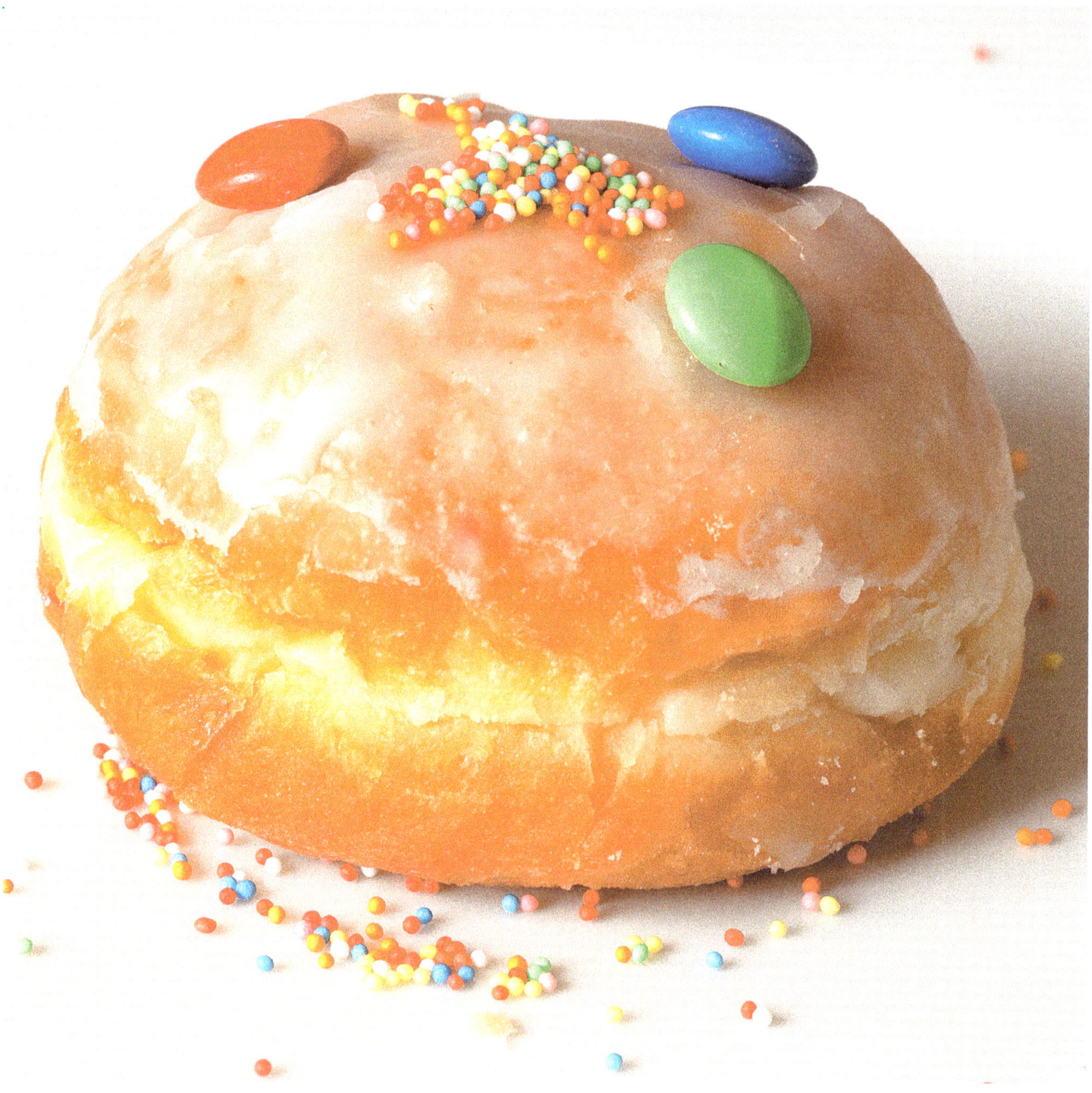

THE BERLIN COOKBOOK

Traditional Recipes and Nourishing Stories

Rose Marie Donhauser

Recipes:
Rose Marie Donhauser

Photos:
Florian Bolk

Translation:
Cindy Opitz

Published 2010 by Berlinica Publishing LLC
255 West 43rd St., Suite 1012, New York, NY, 10036; USA
© 2010 Berlinica Publishing LLC

Cover Photo: Florian Bolk; the photo was taken at the KaDeWe department store.
Bookdesign: Eberhard Delius, Berlin, Germany
Typesetting and Lithography: Reihs Satzstudio, Lohmar, Germany
Printed in the United States of America

All rights reserved under International and Pan-American Copyright Law.
No part of this book may be used or reproduced in any manner whatsoever without written permission except in the case of brief quotations embodied in critical articles and reviews.

ISBN: 978-1-935902-50-8
LCCN: 2010939994

www.Berlinica.com

Photos on pages 1, 2, 9, 11, 12, 13, 14, 19, 25, 26, 29, 31, 31, 32, 35, 39, 40, 43, 44, 45, 50, 51, 52, 53, 55, 62, 67, 69, 71, 72, 76, 78, 80, 82, 83, 85, 86, 89, 91, 93 by Florian Bolk

Photos on pages 15, 16, 17, 18, 20, 21, 22, 46, 48, 56, 57, 60, 65, 75, by Eva C Schweitzer

Photos on pages 23, 37, 58, 59, 61, 73, 87, 90, 92 by Matthias Reihs

Photos on pages 61, 68, 74 by Noah Delius

Table of Contents

Chapter One:
"Lemme grab a bite to eat first"— at home or in the pub...

"Nu lass mir erstma'n Happn essn" **8**

"I love meatballs"
"Buletten — ick liebe dia" **10**

Pickled Eggs, or, Eggs in Brine
Soleier **12**

"Better eat something good, and therefore a little more"
"Lieba wat Jutes. Dafür een bissken mehr" **13**

Crackling Fat on Sliced Bread
Griebenschmalz auf Stulle **14**

Goose-Drippings on Rye Rolls
Schusterjungen mit Gänseschmalz **14**

Seasoned Raw Meatloaf on Bread Rolls
Hackepeter auf Schrippen **15**

Posh "Hackepeter": Minced Steak
Vornehmer Hackepeter: Schabefleisch **15**

Potato Salad with Bockwurst
Kartoffelsalat und Bockwurst **16**

Currywurst with Fries
Currywurst und Fritten **19**

Berlin Döner Kebabs from Kreuzberg
Berliner Döner aus Kreuzberg **20**

Cutlets in Aspic
Sülzkoteletts **22**

Open-Faced Bacon & Egg Sandwiches
Strammer Max **23**

Filleted Pickled Herring
Bismarckheringe **24**

Herring Sauce
Heringsstippe **24**

Rollmops
Rollmops **26**

Fried Pickled Herring
Eingelegte Bratheringe **27**

Chapter Two: Meat and Fish

Green Eel from the Spreewald
Aal grün aus dem Spreewald 28

Old-Berlin-Style Eel
Aal nach Altberliner Art 29

Havel River Zander with Braised Cucumbers
Havelzander mit Schmorgurkengemüse 30

Polish-Style Carp
Karpfen auf polnische Art 33

Crayfish Tails in Dill Sauce
Krebsschwänze in Dillsoße 34

Fried Tench in Dill Butter
Gebratene Schleien in Dillbutter 36

Perch in Beer Sauce
Flussbarsche im Bierteich 36

Holstein-Style Schnitzel
Schnitzel à la Holstein 38

Smoked Pork Loin with Sauerkraut
Kassler auf Sauerkraut 41

Pork Knuckle with Broth
Eisbein mit Brühe 42

Veal Cakes
Kalbsbrisoletten 45

"Faux Rabbit" Meatloaf
"Falscher Hase" 46

Königsberg Meatballs
Klopse aus Königsberg 47

Pan-Fried Berliner Liver
Berliner Leber aus der Pfanne 49

Proud Henry's Thick Bratwursts
Dicke Bratwürste "Stolzer Heinrich" 50

Mother Gerlinde's Beef Roulades
Rinderrouladen von "Mutter Gerlinde" 53

"Dönhoffplatz" Roast Goose
Gänsebraten "Dönhoffplatz" 54

Thick Egg Noodles with Bureaucrat's Sauce
Dicke Eiernudeln mit Beamtenstippe 56

Leftover Hash Hoppelpoppel – Happen-Pappen 57

Rutabaga Stew
Steckrübeneintopf 58

Pea Soup with Ears and Snouts
Löffelerbsen mit Ohren und Schnauzen 59

Emperor Wilhelm II's Potato Soup Kartoffelsuppe "Kaiser Wilhelm II" 60

Aunt Hannelore's Lentil Stew
Linsensuppe von Tante Hannelore 61

Grandpa Lothar's Stuffed Cabbage Leaves
Kohlrouladen nach Opa Lothar 63

Not-So-Elegant Chicken Fricassee
Nicht so vornehmes Hühnerfrikassee 64

Chapter Three:
"Gimme plenty potatoes, but easy on the veggies"

"Jib man ordentlich Kartoffeln – aber spar mit's Jemüse"

Mashed Potatoes
Quetschkartoffeln 66

Potato Purée
Kartoffelpüree 68

Berlin Broth Potatoes
Berliner Brühkartoffeln 68

Potato Pancakes
Kartoffelpuffer 69

Home Fries with Bacon, Onions, and Egg
Bratkartoffeln mit Speck, Zwiebeln und Ei 70

Eggs with Mustard Sauce
Eier mit Mostrichsauce 72

Puréed Peas
Erbspüree 73

Teltow Turnips
Teltower Rübchen 74

Kale
Grünkohl 75

Braised Cucumbers
Schmorgurkengemüse 77

Chapter Four: Desserts

Jelly Donuts (Berliners)
Pfannkuchen 79

Cameroons
Kameruner 80

"Shoe-Sole" Pastries
Blätterteiggebäck "Schuhsohlen" 81

Love Bones
Liebesknochen 82

Bee Stings
Bienenstich 84

Crumb Cake and Coffee with Chickory
Streuselkuchen und Muckefuck 86

Marzipan-Rhubarb Crumb Cake
Marzipankuchen mit Rhabarber und Streuseln 88

Apple Crumb Cake
Apfelstreuselkuchen 90

Red Fruit Pudding with Werder Fruits
Rote Grütze mit Früchten aus Werder 91

"Berlin Air" with Red Berries
"Berliner Luft" mit roten Beeren 92

Index 94

About the Author 95

Chapter One

"Lemme grab a bite to eat first"—at home or in the pub... "Nu lass mir erstma'n Happn essn"

Berlin has always been a place to enjoy great beer. In the Golden Twenties, there were over two hundred breweries; today there are barely half a dozen in the city, including Kindl, Schultheiss, and Radeberger. But every corner bar still serves beer from the keg. There's also a specialty beer that is served in bottles and only available in Berlin: Berliner Weisse. This top-fermented wheat beer with a lower alcohol content originally came to the city from Hamburg at the end of the 16th century.

Bartenders serve **Berliner Weisse "mit Schuss"** (with a shot) of something red or green—a shot of raspberry or woodruff syrup (Waldmeistersirup) poured into a special glass (shaped like a bowl on a stem), which is then filled with weissbier. This red or green beer drink is served with a straw. There's also the **"Berliner Weisse Spezial,"** which is a small glass of red wine mixed with 1 teaspoon sugar and 2 tablespoons lemon juice, to which Berliner Weisse is added.

Or the **"Berliner Weisse Spezial-Flip"**—1 egg yolk and 1 teaspoon sugar mixed with a glass of brandy, topped with Berliner Weisse.

And because beer increases the appetite and the effects of alcohol are somewhat tempered by solid food, most bars also serve a little something to eat.

Many dishes in Berlin cuisine, which is basically simple and down-to-earth, come from the Huguenots, Protestant refugees from France who settled in Prussia in the 17th century. The Huguenots brought many foods to Mark-Brandenburg soil, which were not yet known in Berlin: pork, carp, and goose, for example, along with legumes like lentils, beans, and peas. The Huguenots also brought the "Bulette," along with its name—they called them "Boule," which means (meat)balls.

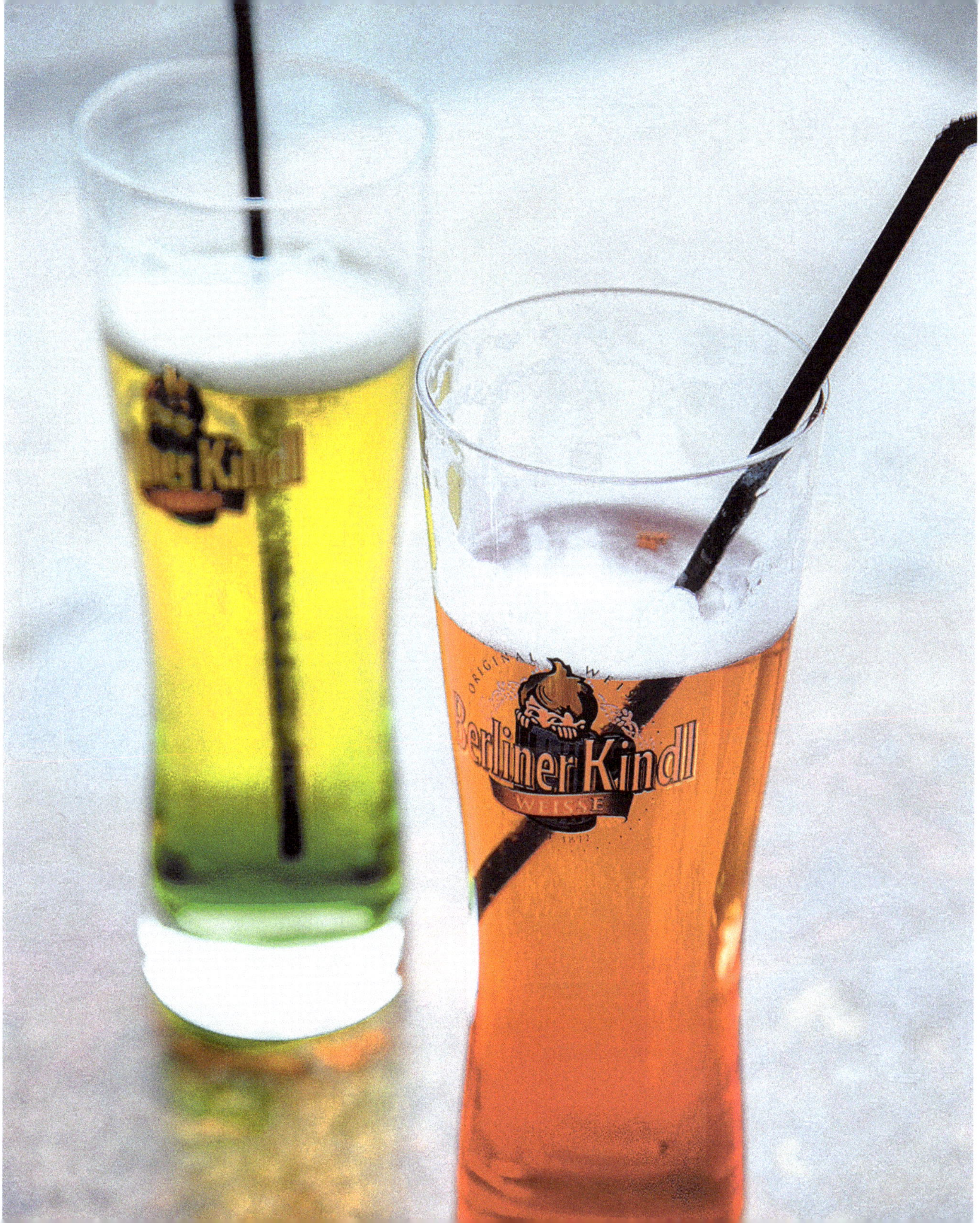
ORIGINAL
Berliner Kindl
WEISSE

"I love Meatballs"

"Buletten — ick liebe dia"

Makes 4 servings:

1 pound of a mixture of ground beef and ground pork (or just ground pork)
2 rolls (1 to 2 days old), sliced or in strips
1 large onion
1 tablespoon fresh, chopped parsley
2 small eggs
salt, pepper

In the frying pan:
about 8 tablespoons vegetable oil
1 tablespoon butter

1. Place the bread strips in a bowl and pour in about 1 cup of lukewarm water, cover with a dish cloth. Peel and dice the onion.

2. Knead the ground meat with the eggs, parsley, and the softened bread. Season with salt and pepper. With damp hands, form the mixture into about 8 balls, then flatten them partially.

3. Heat the vegetable oil in a large pan and brown both sides of the meatballs well. Turn the heat down to medium and fry for another 10 or 15 minutes, adding the butter during this time.

Tip: Remove the meatballs from the pan and let them drain on paper towels. Best served with potato salad, rolls, and mustard.

Tip: The "mushier" the softened bread, the lighter the meatballs will be. The harder the bread is, the firmer the meatballs' consistency will be—but that's a matter of taste in Berlin, or, in the spirit of Prussian king Friedrich II, a.k.a. "Old Fritz," "Everyone should pursue his own path to happiness."

"Buletten," also known as meat "Frikadellen," are made of ground meat mixed with softened "Brötchen" (bread rolls), and are one of Berlin's favorite dishes. Served hot or cold, with a pickle, with or without mustard, eaten plain by hand or on a "Schrippe" (another word for roll)—"ejal" (doesn't matter)—as long as it tastes like mother's. They're served in corner bars, at snack stands, or at home. In one variation, they're called "Pferdeäppel auf Heu" (Road Apples on Hay)—meatballs served over sauerkraut—and in another, they're "naturlemeng"—with fried potatoes.

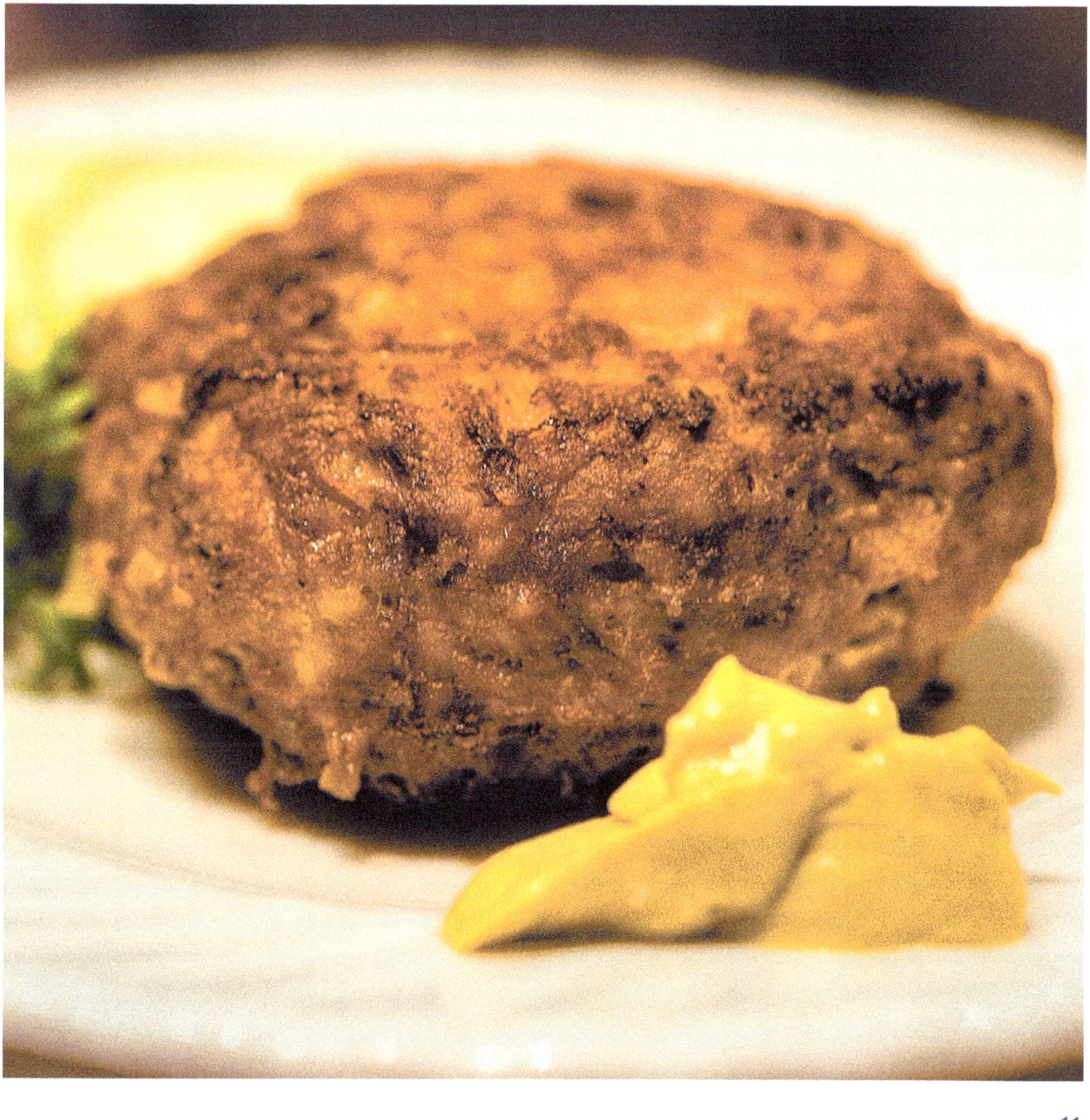

Pickled Eggs, or, Eggs in Brine

Soleier

Halle, home of the salt industry and salt-makers, is also the original source of "Soleier." "Sole" is an antiquated word for brine. Workers used to hang boiled eggs in nets in the simmering brine to eat with their noonday bread.

Berlin developed a taste for eggs in brine, which began showing up in pubs because they were easy to eat and went well with beer. Tall jars, like candy jars, also called "Hungertürme" (hunger towers), still stand on bar counters today, containing eggs soaking in brine. Hungry patrons pop one or two (or three) eggs from the jar, tap them against the table, peel and cut them in half, add a thick layer of mustard, some salt, and a little pepper, and knock 'em back...

Makes 4 eggs:

4 large, fresh eggs
1 cup water
1 teaspoon salt
2 bay leaves

1 Boil the eggs until hard (for about 10 minutes), douse in cold water, and tap lightly on all sides.

2 Add salt and bay leaves to the water and return to a boil, then turn down to medium heat and let steep for 5 minutes. Let stand until completely cool.

3 Place the eggs in a tall container and add the cooled liquid, covering the eggs completely. Let stand in a cool place for at least 24 hours.

Before serving, remove the eggs from the brine, knock them against a hard surface, and peel.

"Better eat something good, and therefore a little more"

"Lieba wat Jutes. Dafür een bissken mehr"

Berlin has starved more than once; a piece of bread was a luxury before and after both world wars. This explains Berlin's strong love of the "Butterstulle" (buttered slice of bread). Even today, Berlin residents will hoard food with a mischievous grin, "You never know when the Russians will come." The "Butterstulle" consists of a slice of classic sourdough bread of wheat and rye, spread with butter. One variation is the "Beamten-Schiebewurst" (bureaucrat's sausage push): A buttered slice of bread with a little piece of sausage on the edge. With each bite of bread, the sausage is moved around the slice, such that each bite of bread is accompanied by at least a tiny bit of meat. The last bite of sausage is saved for the last bite of bread. The best way to eat bread in Berlin, however, is piled thick with sliced boiled eggs, ham, cheese, or sausage. It's also served in the "Klappstulle" (sandwich) style, a hefty layer between two slices of buttered bread. This explains the Berlin expression, "Wennde pampich wirst, denn nehm ick dir uff de Stulle und denne wirste mitjefressen als Belach" (if you talk back, I'll put you on a slice of bread and eat you as the topping).

Crackling Fat on Sliced Bread

Griebenschmalz auf Stulle

Raw, fatty bacon—well rendered (a Berlin specialty)—is a staple at Kirmes and Christmas markets. Spread this specialty on thick slices (Stullen) of rustic bread, and you've got yourself a "Schmalzstulle."

You can get fresh, finely minced pork fat in small plastic containers at the butcher's. You can also make your own, using pork bacon.

Makes 4 servings:

1 pound raw pork bacon, without the rind
2 fresh sprigs marjoram

1 Chop a piece of pork bacon into small cubes. Render (fry the fat out) together with the marjoram in a wide pot for about 40 minutes. The fat will become clear and form small, brown greaves.

2 Put the clear fat and greaves in a small crock, chill, and let solidify until spreadable. Serve with salt and pepper on fresh peasant-style rye bread.

Goose-Drippings on Rye Rolls

Schusterjungen mit Gänseschmalz

"Schusterjungen" (literally "cobblers' apprentices") are crusty rolls, also known as "Salzkuchen" (salt cakes). They're irregular in shape and made of a blend of half rye flour and half wheat flour, with sourdough. They go well with pub meals, especially with goose-drippings or crackling fat and Harzer cheese (sour-milk cheese from the Harz region).

Makes 4 servings:

1 pound goose lard (fresh goose fat)
1 large onion
1 tart apple (e.g., Boskop, Braeburn, Granny Smith)
1 tablespoon fresh mugwort (wormwood) leaves
salt
Serve with 8 rye rolls, fresh from the oven

1 Chop the goose fat as finely as possible and render down with about ½ cup water in a wide pot. (Fry over medium heat until the fat runs clear.)

2 Peel and mince the onion. Peel, quarter, core, and dice the apple.

3 Add the minced onion to the clear fat and fry until golden. Remove the pot from the stove; stir in the diced apple and mugwort; and transfer to a small crock or stoneware pot. Chill and allow to congeal.

Tip: Cut the rolls in half and spread with goose-dripping.

Seasoned Raw Meatloaf on Bread Rolls

Hackepeter auf Schrippen

Makes 4 servings:

1 pound ground pork
1 large onion, finely chopped
salt
freshly ground pepper
Serve on fresh rolls

1 Knead the ground pork together with the chopped onion, seasoning liberally with salt and pepper.

2 Spread the mixture on fresh rolls and—viola! Garnish with lettuce or sliced cucumbers, onions, or tomatoes.

Posh "Hackepeter": Minced Steak

Vornehmer Hackepeter: Schabefleisch

Those who can afford to use steak when making seasoned raw meatloaf have got it good. "Normal" Berliners eat "Hackepeter" (seasoned raw meatloaf), and "posh" Berliners eat "Schabefleisch" (minced steak), made from finer (and more expensive) beef cuts, like sirloin or fillet mignon, run through the meat grinder.

Makes 4 servings:

1½ pounds ground chuck
4 fresh egg yolks
8 anchovies (from a tin)
2 tablespoons pickled capers
1 large, chopped onion

Serve with:
salt, pepper
paprika
caraway
Worcestershire sauce
1 small jar pickles

1 With damp hands, form ground chuck into several balls, place them on a plate, and press a hollow into the center of each. Place an egg yolk in each depression and lay two anchovies on top, forming a cross.

2 Place the ingredients on the table, so each person can mix his own minced steak.

Tip: Berliners enjoy toast with this dish (toasted slices of white bread).

Potato Salad with Bockwurst

Kartoffelsalat und Bockwurst

Bockwurst was invented in Berlin in 1889 by Richard Scholtz, who ran a sausage stand on Spreewaldplatz in the Kreuzberg district. Small sausages like wieners or frankfurters had already been around for a while, but Scholtz created a huge sausage for boiling, almost a foot long. The origin of the name "Bockwurst" isn't clear, with several possible explanations: maybe because it was as large as a young billy-goat (Geißbock), or because it was as filling as dark Bock beer. Or maybe Scholtz didn't like the Berlin saying, "Mensch, eh der 'Wurscht' sagt, ha'ck se schon vadrückt!" ("It takes him longer to say 'Wurst' than to eat one.")—so Scholtz came up with a sausage large enough to defy the expression.

Makes 4 servings:
- 1½ pounds potatoes, equally sized
- 4 hard-boiled eggs
- 4 dill pickles
- 2 egg yolks
- 1 teaspoon hot mustard
- ½ cup vegetable oil
- 2 tablespoons white wine vinegar
- salt, pepper
- 2 tablespoons chopped parsley

Serve with:
- 4 hot Bockwursts (heat in a pot of water)
- 4 bread rolls
- hot or honey mustard

1. Boil the potatoes (skins on) until tender; drain, peel, and slice. Peel the eggs and dice (slice length-wise and width-wise, using an egg slicer). Dice the pickles, too.

2. Using an electric hand mixer, mix the 2 egg yolks with the mustard; add the vegetable oil, a little at a time, forming a creamy mayonnaise.

3. Season the mayonnaise with the white wine vinegar, salt, and pepper; carefully mix with the other ingredients in a large bowl.

Sprinkle with parsley, or mix the parsley into the other ingredients. Distribute the potato salad onto plates and place a Bockwurst on each. Serve with rolls and mustard.

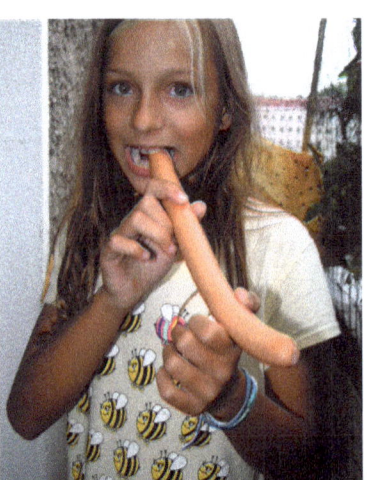

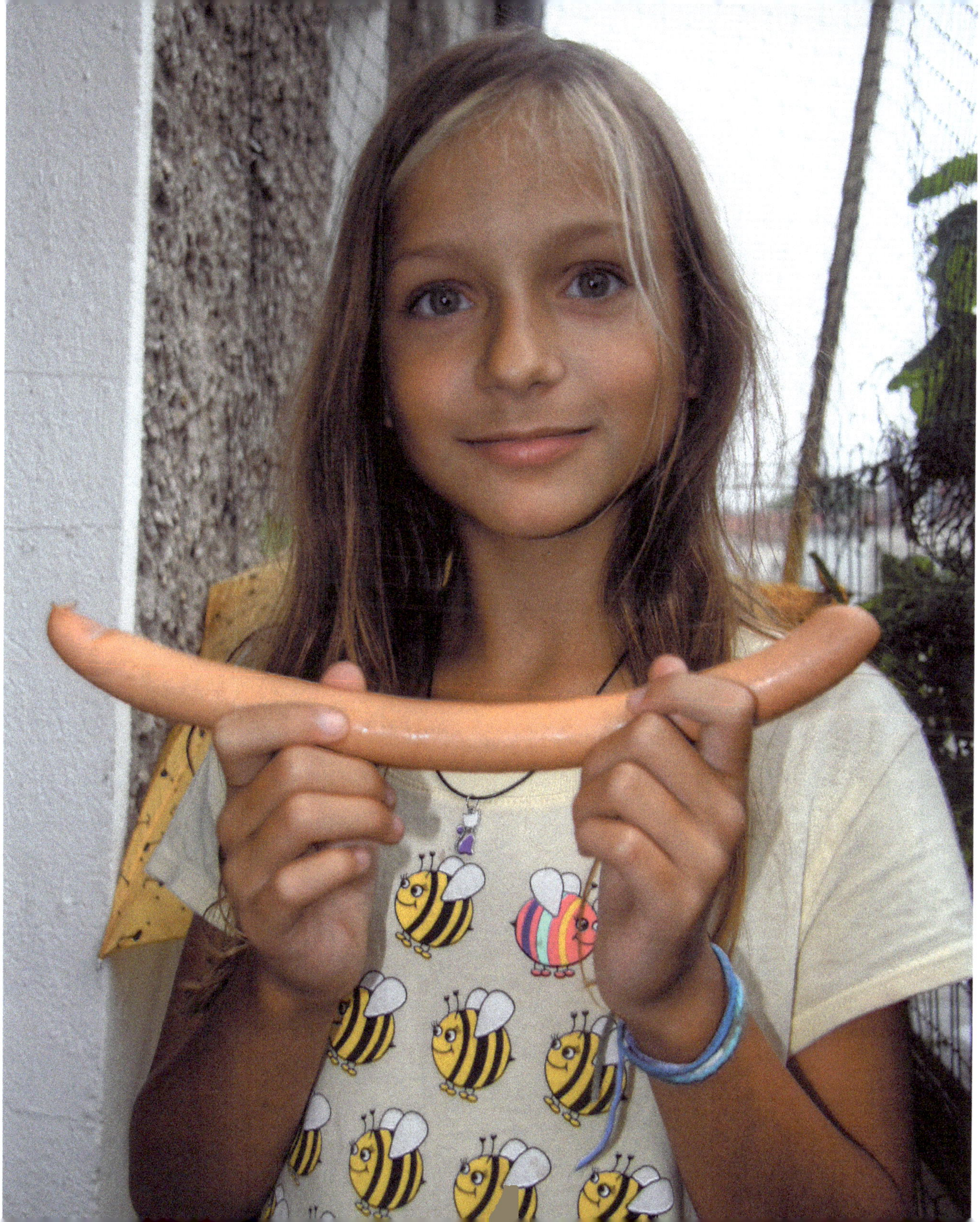

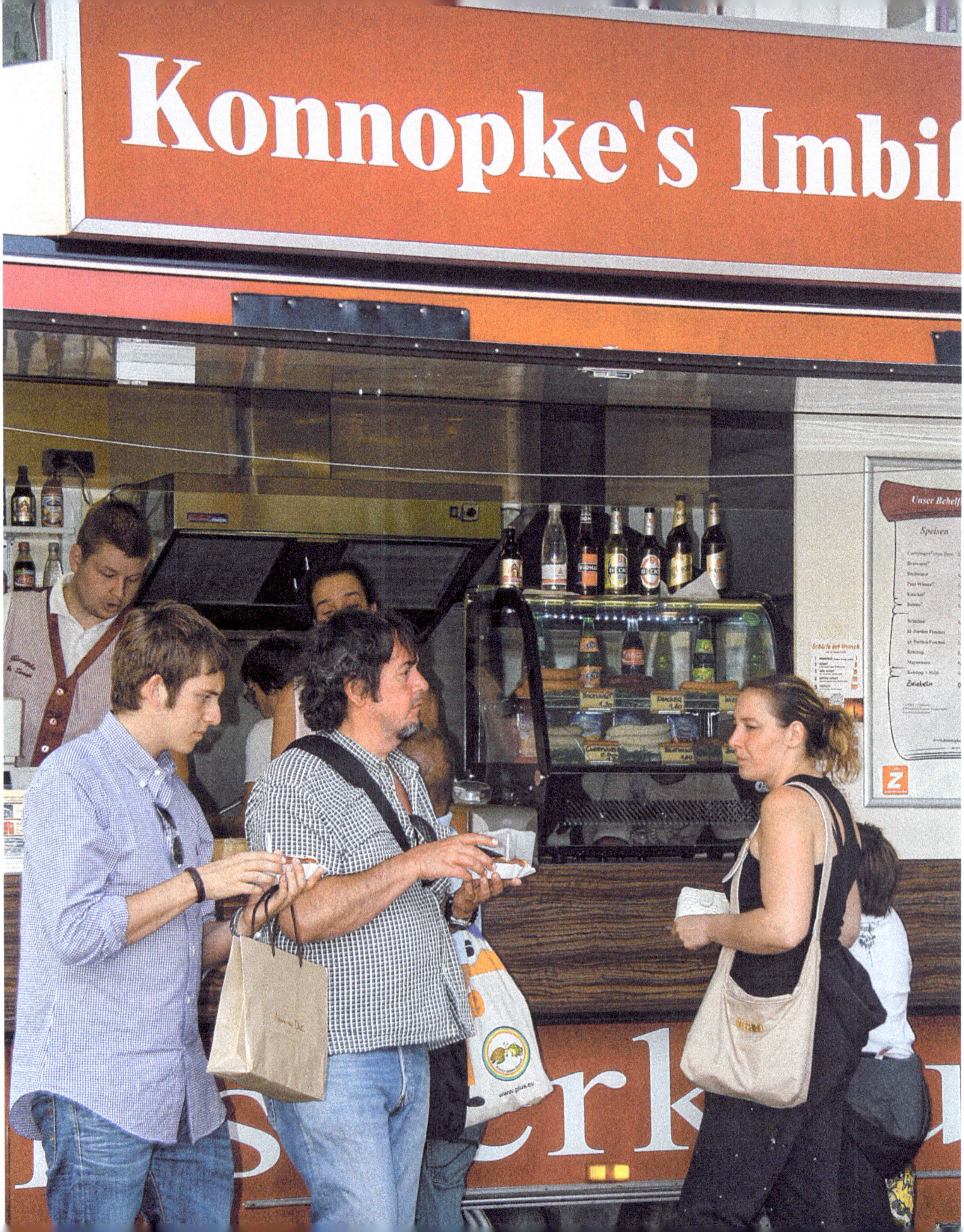
Konnopke's
Speisen

Currywurst with Fries

Currywurst und Fritten

You can't visit Berlin and not eat Currywurst—"jet jar nich" ("that just won't do"). The magic of Currywurst remains a culinary hit, and the average Berliner at the neighborhood fry shack loves to discuss where to find the best curry stands. Each and every Berliner, however, claims to know where the best one is—though this usually has something to do with how close the stand is to his way home.

Herta Heuwer, the former owner of a snack stand on the corner of Kantstraße and Kaiser-Friedrich-Straße, is credited with inventing Currywurst. On September 4, 1949, she served grilled, boiled sausage with a sauce made from tomato paste, curry powder, Worcestershire sauce, and a few secret ingredients.

A commemorative plaque honors Herta Heuwer and her invention, right where her stand once stood. Soon many sausage-shop owners were joining the Currywurst bandwagon and coming up with their own secret blends of curry, ketchup, and spices, along with a secret ingredient or two. In East Berlin, Waltraud Ziervogel's stand was the most famous spot for Currywurst, the "Konnopke," which she opened in 1976, under the elevated railway on Schönhauser Allee in Prenzlauer Berg.

Without a doubt, Currywurst knocked Bockwurst, beloved in the postwar years, from the top spot. Currywurst with fries are best eaten at a stand, in a bar, or in the little pub on the corner, among like-minded neighbors, with "ne Molle" (a glass of beer) and a thick napkin to wipe away any dribbled sauce. There's just one unresolved question among Berliners, "Would you like your wurst with or without the casing?"

A recipe (sort of):

4 grilled or fried bratwursts
A generous amount of tomato ketchup
curry powder to taste
18 ounces golden-fried French fries

Place the brats on plates, cut diagonally into small slices, spoon ketchup over the top, arrange the fries around the edges, and dust everything with curry powder.

Berlin Döner Kebabs from Kreuzberg

Berliner Döner aus Kreuzberg

In Berlin, there are more döner kebab stands per capita than in Istanbul. A lot more, even, because there are no döner kebab stands in Istanbul, because they're a Berlin invention. In 1971, Kreuzberg resident Kadir Nurman, an employee at the Zoo train station's City-Imbiss, found a way to turn the Turkish dish "Döner Kebap," usually served on a plate, into a handheld meal, by packing it into flatbread for Berliners on the go. His great idea soon enabled him to go into business for himself. Since then, the döner kebab Berliners can eat on their way home, has become just as much a part of the snack-stand scene as Currywurst. "The döner kebab is Berlin's favorite snack," Kadir Nurman has observed. Berliners would probably never think of making döner kebabs in their own homes, but it's easy. This recipe is four servings, calculated generously because, as those who've had a döner kebab from a Turkish grill know, just one fills you up for the whole day.

Makes 4 servings:

1½ pounds lean veal
salt
Freshly ground pepper
½ teaspoon ground cumin (or a prepared döner-kebab seasoning)
2 small onions
5 tablespoons olive oil
4 cloves garlic
¾ cup sheep-milk yogurt
1 tablespoon fresh chopped parsley
4 flatbreads (the size of your hand)

Garnishes:
2 tomatoes
1 cup red cabbage
1 cup cucumber (grated)
1 onion

Other: **4 grill skewers**

1 Preheat the oven to 430 degrees (grill setting). Cut the veal into thin slices and season with salt, pepper, and cumin. Place the seasoned meat on the four skewers.

2 Peel the onions and grate finely. Stir half of the resulting onion paste with the olive oil and brush onto the skewered meat, coating all sides.

3 Place the skewers on a grid on the middle rack of the preheated oven. Grill for about 20 minutes, turning several times.

4 In the meantime, peel and press the garlic into the yogurt, using a garlic press. Stir in the parsley, and season with salt and pepper. Set sauce aside.

5 Slice the flatbreads in half, but not all the way through, to form pockets. Drizzle a little olive oil into the pockets. Wash and dice the tomatoes.

6 Wash the red cabbage and cut into thin strips. Wash the cucumber and grate finely. Peel and halve the onion, and cut into very thin strips. Arrange the prepared ingredients on a serving platter.

During the meat's last 5 to 8 minutes under the grill, warm the flatbread on the oven floor.

7 Remove the skewers and the flatbread from the oven. Remove the meat from each skewer and place in a bread pocket. Add all of the remaining ingredients or just some, according to taste, and dribble the garlic sauce over the top. Döner kebabs can also be served on plates with rice and a salad.

Cutlets in Aspic

Sülzkoteletts

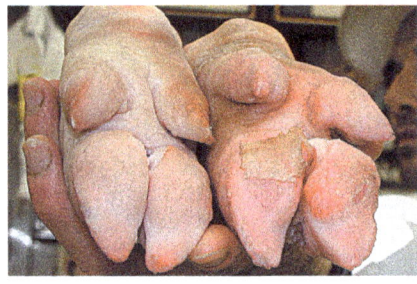

"*Sülzkoteletts*" are cutlets prepared in aspic, which is made from clarified stock containing gelatinous bits of meat. Cooks used to preserve leftover meat with pickles and eggs this way, as gelatin will keep up to a week in the refrigerator. It was also considered a handy meal at a bar, pulled from the fridge and placed on a plate for a guest. A man's meal—one that goes well with beer.

Makes 4 servings:

**2 pounds calves' and pigs' feet (order both from the butcher, cut into pieces)
salt
½ bunch soup vegetables (1 carrot, 1 leek, 1 stalk celery)
1 small onion
5 tablespoons white wine vinegar
2 bay leaves
several peppercorns
2 cloves
1 sprig fresh marjoram
4 pork chops
1 boiled egg
1 dill pickle**

Other: **4 plastic gelatin molds**

1 Wash calves' and pigs' feet thoroughly and place in a large pot. Add about 8 cups water, a dash of salt, and bring to a boil. Reduce the heat and skim the foam from the surface with a skimmer.

2 Wash the carrots, leek, and celery; peel the onion and chop vegetables into small pieces. Add these to the pot, along with the white wine vinegar, bay leaves, peppercorns, cloves, and marjoram. Simmer approximately 1½ hours. Place the pork chops in the broth for the last 30 minutes.

3 Place the cooked pork chops on a plate. Strain the contents of the pot through a fine sieve and boil several more minutes; season with white wine vinegar, if desired.

4 Peel the egg and chop with an eggslicer. Slice the pickle.

5 Pour some of the liquid into gelatin molds, covering the bottoms, and place them in the refrigerator to solidify (this does not take long). Remove the forms from the refrigerator and place a pork chop in each, followed by the sliced egg and pickle. Cover with the remaining liquid and place in the refrigerator to chill overnight, or for at least four hours.

Tip: Dip the molds in hot water and turn them over onto plates. Serve with fried potatoes.

Open-Faced Bacon & Egg Sandwiches

Strammer Max

"*Ick fall jleich um vor Hunger*" ("I'm about to keel over from hunger")—those who talk like that might also order a "Strammer Max," a kind of open-faced sandwich. Large, scrumptious, with the bread hanging off the edge of the plate and the eggs soooo huge—ostrich-sized, if you please—that's the way Berliners like it. In Berlin, a good restaurant is one that serves large portions.

Makes 4 servings:

4 thick slices bread
2 tablespoons butter, at room temperature
1 cup diced raw bacon
8 eggs
3 tablespoons cooking oil
salt, pepper

Garnish with:
2 tablespoons fresh, chopped parsley
2 tomatoes, quartered
Fresh cucumber slices

1 Spread butter on each slice of bread; place each on a plate and sprinkle with diced ham.

2 Fry the eggs in the cooking oil and remaining butter, and place two fried eggs on each slice of bread. Season with salt and pepper, and garnish with tomato, cucumber, and parsley.

Filleted Pickled Herring

Bismarckheringe

Imperial Chancellor Otto von Bismarck, who united Germany in the 19th century, once said to Parliament, "If herring were as rare as caviar or lobster, it would be considered a delicacy," and, "If herring cost a dollar, people would say it tastes better." Because of these auspicious utterances, resourceful fishmonger Friedrich Wiechmann of Stralsund sent the chancellor a barrel of pickled Baltic Sea herring for his birthday. To show his gratitude, the chancellor gave Wiechmann permission to call that kind of herring "Bismarck Herring" from then on.

Makes 4 servings:

- 12 green (raw), herring fillets (ask the fish shop to prepare them)
- 4 tablespoons salt
- 2 cups dry white wine
- 2 cups water
- 1 cup white wine vinegar
- 1 teaspoon sugar
- 2 large onions
- 2 carrots
- 5 bay leaves
- 2 tablespoons peppercorns
- 2 tablespoons allspice

1. Rinse the herring under cold running water and pat dry with paper towels. Rub with salt, cover with foil, and chill in the refrigerator for at least 2 hours.

2. In the meantime, bring the white wine, water, vinegar, and sugar to a boil. Chill completely. Peel the onions and slice into thin rings. Peel and slice the carrots.

3. Rinse the herring and pat dry again. Layer the fish with the sliced onions and carrots, bay leaves, peppercorns, and allspice in a jar or crock. Fill the jar with the chilled brine, covering everything completely. Close the jar with foil and let stand in a cool place for at least 2 days.

Tip: Remove the pickled herring from the jar, wipe, and divide onto plates. Serve with fresh onion slices, sweet pickles, and boiled potatoes (leave skins on).

Herring Sauce

Heringsstippe

Makes 4 servings:

- 12 Bismarck herring fillets (see recipe: filleted pickled herring)
- 3 small, tart apples (e.g. Boskop, Braeburn, Granny Smith)
- 3 medium onions
- 3 pickles
- 1 cup mayonnaise
- 1 cup sour cream
- 5 tablespoons milk
- salt, pepper
- 1 teaspoon sugar

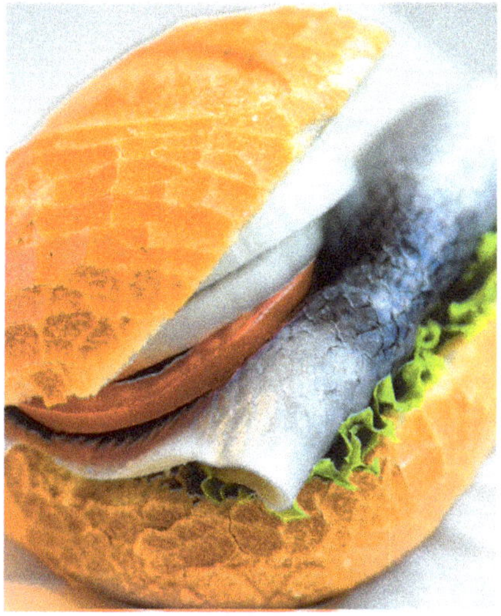

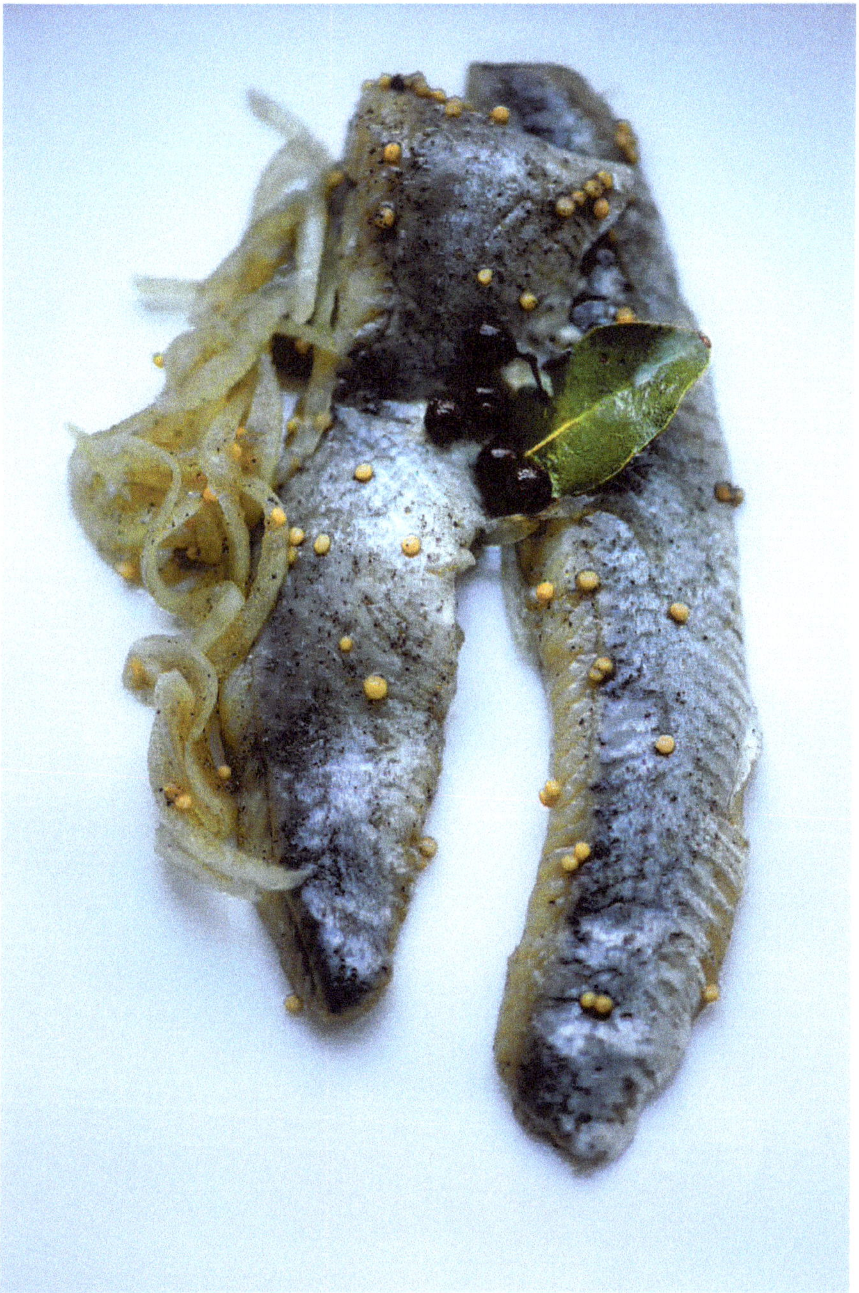

1 Remove the Bismarck herring from the brine, rinse, and pat dry with paper towels. Slice diagonally into strips.

2 Wash the apples (do not peel), remove the cores, and dice. Peel and dice the onions; dice the pickles as well.

3 Stir the mayonnaise with sour cream and milk until creamy, and season with salt, pepper, and sugar. Carefully combine with the prepared ingredients and season once more to taste.

Tip: Serve with course, whole-grain bread with butter and boiled potatoes (leave skin on).

Cucumbers grow in Brandenburg, especially in the Spreewald.

Rollmops

Rollmops

A variation of the previous dish is called rollmops, which calls for headless, deboned herring pickled in salt. Berliners like to leave the "tail" on their herring, to make them easier to pick up and eat by hand, and because it reminds them of the "mops," a pug dog breed, the favorite lapdog of the "Wilmersdorf Widows"— conservative old ladies from the bourgeois West Berlin district of Wilmersdorf, immortalized in the Berlin musical Linie 1 *(Line #1)*, about the subway running from Charlottenburg to Kreuzberg.

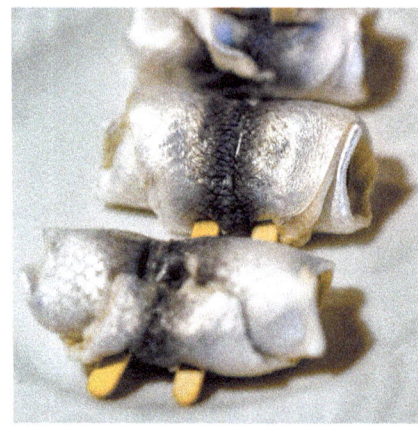

Makes 4 servings:

12 salted herring fillets (Matjes fillets, packed in oil)
2 tablespoons medium-hot mustard
2 dill pickles
1 onion
1 tablespoon marinated capers
1 teaspoon peppercorns
2 cups water
1 cup white wine vinegar
2 bay leaves
1 dash sugar

Other: **toothpicks**

1 Rinse the salted herring under cold running water, pat dry with paper towels, and arrange on a work surface. Spread a thin layer of mustard on each. Slice pickles into thin strips. Peel the onion and cut into thin strips. Cover the fish fillets with the onion and pickle strips, and sprinkle with capers and peppercorns. Roll the herring and secure with toothpicks.

2 Bring the water, vinegar, bay leaves, and sugar to a boil; chill completely.

3 Layer the rollmops in a crock and cover with the chilled brine. Cover and let stand for at least 24 hours.

Tip: Rollmops is a typical pub dish, which "absorbs" alcohol. Serve with bread and butter or rye rolls.

Fried Pickled Herring

Eingelegte Bratheringe

Makes 4 to 6 servings:

2 pounds herring fillets
juice of 1 lemon
salt
freshly ground pepper
3 tablespoons flour
2 tablespoons vegetable oil
4 tablespoons clarified butter
1 cup white wine vinegar
1 cup water
½ teaspoon peppercorns
½ teaspoon coriander seeds
1 teaspoon mustard seeds
2 bay leaves
2 large onions
1 pickled cucumber

1. Rinse the herring under cold running water and pat dry with paper towels. Sprinkle with lemon juice, season with salt and pepper, and dredge in flour.

2. Heat vegetable oil and clarified butter in a large pan, and fry the herring on both sides, for total time of about 20 minutes, until brown and crispy. Remove the herring from the pan and place on paper towels to drain and cool.

3. Bring the vinegar, water, and spices to a boil; chill completely.

4. Peel the onions and cut into thin strips. Slice the pickle.

5. Layer the cooled herring with the onion strips and sliced pickle in a crock or stoneware pot. Pour the chilled marinade over the top, cover, and let stand in a cool place for at least 24 hours.

Tip: Remove the fried salted herrings from the marinade and serve with fried potatoes.

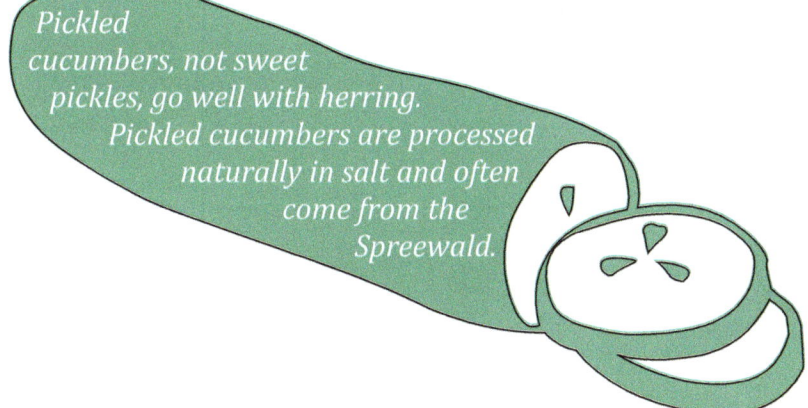

Pickled cucumbers, not sweet pickles, go well with herring. Pickled cucumbers are processed naturally in salt and often come from the Spreewald.

Chapter Two: Meat and Fish

Green Eel from the Spreewald

Aal grün aus dem Spreewald

With its diverse flora and fauna, the Spreewald is one of the most well-known areas in southern Brandenburg's Niederlausitz region. The Spreewald is famous for punt-boat rides, beginning at the little town of Lübben. Using long poles, like in Venice, fishermen push their punts through the countless canals and arms of the Spree River, also called "Fließe" (flows), which wind through the landscape. As early as 600 AD, the Sorbs, also known as Wends, settled the land. Many of their traditions, costumes, and customs have survived through the centuries. Among them is agriculture, which produces the famous and diverse cucumbers and horseradish. The Spreewald is also known for its fish specialties. Eel is especially loved here. In many traditional restaurants, this rarity is still served today in its original form, with small boiled potatoes and cucumber salad, with cucumbers from the Spreewald.

Makes 4 servings:

2 pounds deboned, skinned eel from the Spree River
salt, black pepper
2 tablespoons white wine vinegar
4 sprigs dill
1 onion
1 cup dry white wine
3 bay leaves
6 tablespoons butter
1 tablespoon flour
1 cup cream
1 dash sugar
juice of ½ lemon
1 egg yolk

Serve with:

4 tablespoons fresh, chopped dill

1. Cut the eel into two-inch chunks and season with salt and pepper. Sprinkle with vinegar and let marinate several minutes.

2. In the meantime, wash the dill and chop coarsely. Wash the onion (do not peel), and cut into small pieces. Bring 2 cups water and the white wine to boil in a pot. Add the dill, onion pieces, and bay leaves, and reduce the heat.

3. Place the chunks of eel in the simmering brine and simmer over medium heat until tender, 15 to 20 minutes. Remove the eel with a slotted spoon and place on a plate. Strain the brine through a fine sieve.

4. In a pan, stir the butter and flour into a blond roux, and add the eel brine, stirring vigorously to remove lumps. Refine

Old-Berlin-Style Eel

Aal nach Altberliner Art

with cream, and season with salt, pepper, sugar, and lemon juice.

5 Turn off the heat. Remove some sauce from the pan and whisk with an egg before returning to the pan and combining with the rest of the sauce. Arrange the eel pieces on a large serving platter and cover with the sauce and generous amounts of fresh, chopped dill.

Season chunks of eel with salt and pepper. Heat 6 tablespoons of butter and a heaping ½ cup of finely grated dry dark rye bread. Add the eel, two bay leaves, and a dozen black peppercorns. Cook on a stove, turning the eel two or three times and slowly adding 2 cups of Berliner weissbier, a little at a time.

Cook on a stove, turning the eel over low heat, covered with a lid, for 15 to 20 minutes, until tender. Remove the eel from the pan and place some on each plate. Season the eel stock to taste, and refine with lemon juice; spoon over the eel.

Havel River Zander with Braised Cucumbers

Havelzander mit Schmorgurkengemüse

Berlin is crisscrossed by many rivers, like the Spree, which flows from the Spreewald, or the Havel, which stretches to the Wannsee, the channeled Panke, and other tributaries and canals, especially the Landwehr Canal. You can travel by boat from Berlin all the way to Brandenburg—from lake to lake—using the many rivers as conduits. There are also fish in Berlin's waterways, the most famous of which is the zander (often called pike-perch).

Makes 4 servings:

4 zander fillets, about ½ pound each
juice of 1 lemon
salt, black pepper
1 pound cucumbers
1 onion
¼ pound bacon
2 tomatoes
4 tablespoons vegetable oil
4 tablespoons clarified butter
2 tablespoons flour, for dredging
1 tablespoon butter
½ cup cream
1 dash sugar
1 dash white wine vinegar
1 tablespoon chopped dill

1. Rinse the fish under cold running water and pat dry with paper towels. Drizzle with lemon juice, and season with salt and pepper. Set aside.

2. Wash and peel the cucumbers, cut lengthwise, and scrape out the seeds with a spoon. Cut each half into thin slices.

3. Peel the onion and mince with the bacon. Blanch the tomatoes, rinse in cold water, remove the stem and seeds, and dice the flesh into small cubes.

4. Heat the vegetable oil in a wide pot and braise the minced bacon and onion. Add the cucumber and cook for 10 minutes, stirring occasionally.

5. Meanwhile, heat the clarified butter in a pan. Dredge the fish in flour and place in the pan. Fry for about 10 minutes, adding the butter to the pan and turning the fish several times.

6. While the fish is frying, season the cucumber mix with salt and pepper, and add the cream. Braise the vegetables over low heat, adding the vinegar and sugar to taste.

7. Add the diced tomatoes, and transfer the vegetables to a serving bowl; garnish generously with dill. Place the fish on plates and spoon pan drippings over them.

Tip: Serve with boiled potatoes tossed in butter.

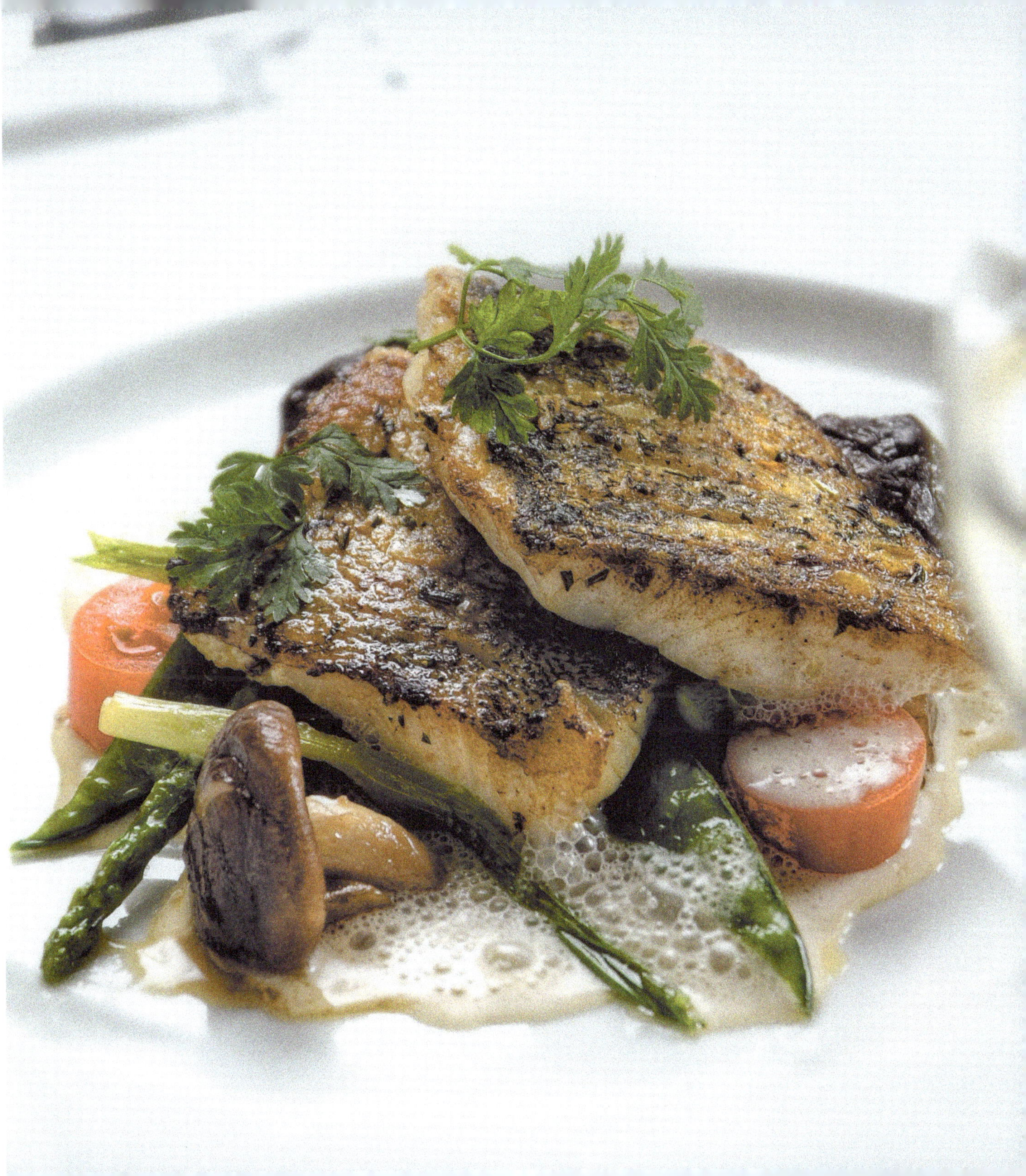

And this, by the way, is how the zander looks while still alive

Polish-Style Carp

Karpfen auf polnische Art

Traditionally, this fish dish is served on holidays. Many families eat carp at Christmas and New Year's. In Berlin, you can buy live carp at fish farms. But beware! Your bathroom or kitchen might turn into a battlefield when it comes time to slaughter the carp, or your children might demand the fish's freedom. When I brought live carp home one Christmas, the container fell over in the trunk of my car. It's best to bring them home pre-prepped.

Makes 4 servings:

1 filleted carp, cut into pieces (prepared by a fishmonger)
juice of 1 lemon
salt, black pepper
½ bunch soup vegetables (1 carrot, 1 leek, 1 celery stalk)
2 small onions
4 tablespoons butter
1 bay leaf
4 cloves
2 cups dark beer
7 tablespoons grated gingersnaps (or commercially prepared Saucenlebkuchen)

1. Rinse the carp under cold running water and pat dry with paper towels. Drizzle with lemon juice and season with salt and pepper.

2. Wash and chop the vegetables. Wash and chop the onion, leaving the skin on. Heat the butter in a tall pan and braise the vegetables. Add bay leaf and season with salt and pepper. Pour in the beer, bring to a brief boil, and stir in the grated gingersnaps (or Saucenlebkuchen).

3. Place the carp in the sauce, cover with a lid, and cook the fish until tender, about 20 minutes. Turn the fish once or twice.

4. Remove the carp and place on plates. Strain the sauce through a fine sieve, season to taste, and spoon over the fish.

Tip: This goes well with boiled potatoes and beer.

Crayfish Tails in Dill Sauce

Krebsschwänze in Dillsoße

Up until the end of the 19th century, the famous "Oderkrebs" (Oder crayfish) were fished from the Oder River by the basketful and rushed from Berlin to Paris on the night train, they were such a delicacy. Berlin waters were so full of their own beautiful crayfish that masters were not allowed to serve "Oderkrebs" to their servants more than three times a week. Many dishes from those days are still served in Berlin, though now the crayfish must be imported, because locally they're nearly extinct. The following is a favorite recipe in Berlin, without shells, for the sake of simplicity.

Makes 4 servings:

20 shelled crayfish
   (try Louisiana crayfish)
juice of ½ lemon
salt, black pepper
2 tablespoons butter
1 teaspoon flour
1 cup fish juice (bottled)
1 cup cream
several dashes Worcestershire
   sauce
1 egg yolk
2 tablespoons chopped dill

1. Drizzle lemon juice on the crayfish tails and season with salt and pepper.

2. Stir the butter and flour into a blond roux and add the fish juice. Stir continuously, to prevent lumps from forming in the sauce; add the cream.

3. Season the sauce with salt, pepper, and Worcestershire sauce; remove some of the sauce to mix with the egg yolk, then return to the pan. Place the crayfish tails in the pan to steep briefly, just 3 to 4 minutes. Stir the dill into the sauce.

Tip: Form a rice border around the edge of the plates, or tip rice from a timbale form onto preheated plates. Ladle sauce into the middle and drape the crayfish tails over the rice.

Variations:

Live crayfish are seldom available; you're more likely to find them pre-cooked or refrigerated or frozen in the shell. Warm and season cold or thawed crayfish (24 pieces) in a large pot with 2 cups dry white wine, 4 cups water, 1 lemon peel, 2 cloves, 5 white peppercorns, 2 dill sprigs, and 1 minced shallot. Cover with a lid and let steep about 5 minutes. Strain the broth through a sieve and add to the sauce as described above.

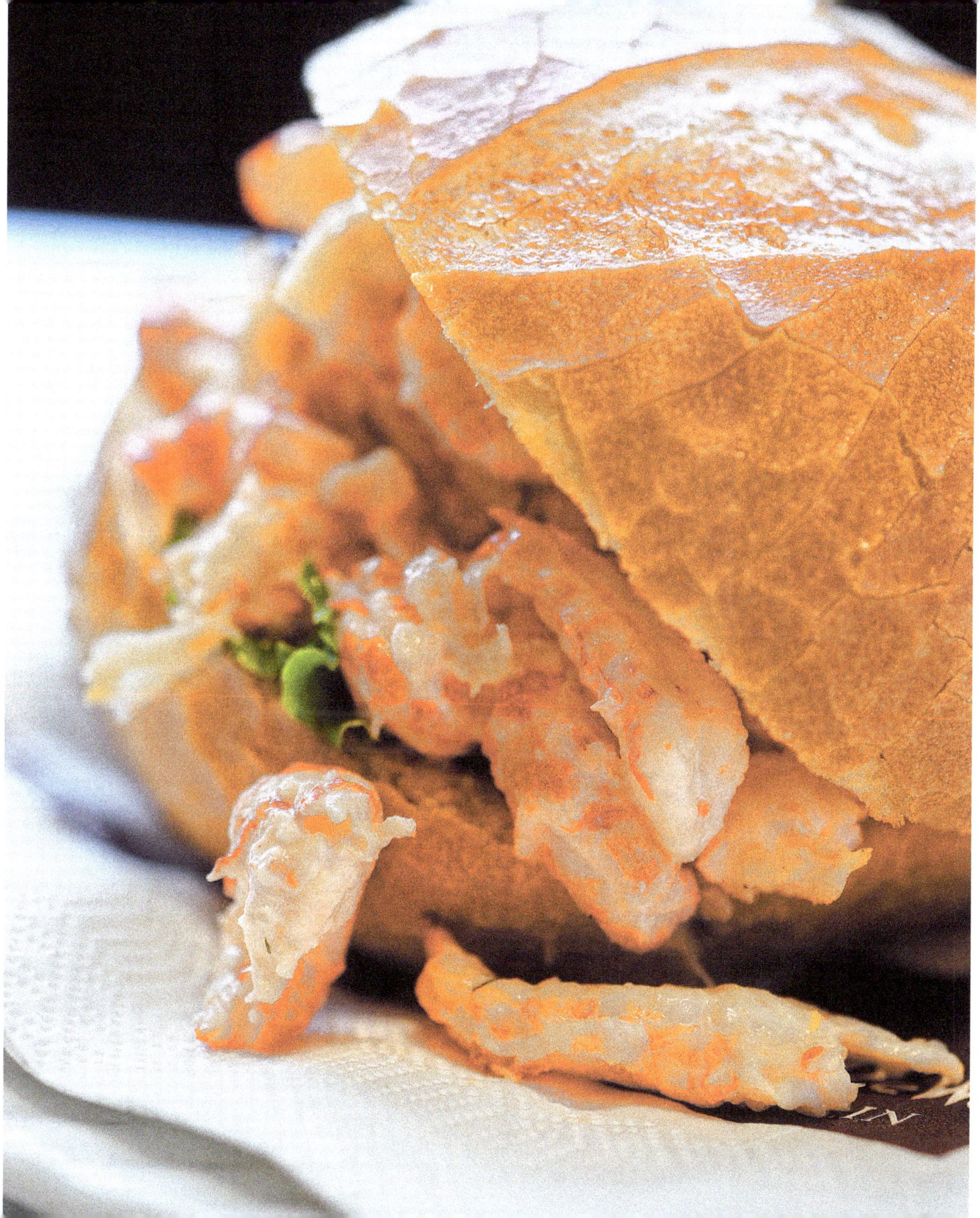

Fried Tench in Dill Butter

Gebratene Schleien in Dillbutter

Not only are there many lakes and rivers within city limits, but Berlin is also surrounded by lakes. And "Berlin's Bathtub" lies a hundred miles to the north—Usedom, the Baltic Sea Island, and the island of Rügen. These outlying areas also provide many fish that are served in Berlin.

Makes 4 servings:

4 tenches, about 1 pound each (or substitute carp)
juice of 1 lemon
salt, black pepper
½ bunch dill
¼ cup vegetable oil
½ cup flour
4 tablespoons butter

1 Rinse the tenches under cold running water and pat dry with paper towels. Drizzle with lemon juice and season with salt and pepper.

2 Rinse the dill, pat dry, and remove the leaves from the stems. Place ⅓ inside the fish and finely chop the rest. Heat the vegetable oil in a large pan.

3 Dredge the fish in flour, tapping to remove extra flour, and place in the pan. Fry about 20 minutes, turning several times; add the butter.

4 Place the fried fish on preheated plates. Add the dill to the pan drippings and drizzle over the fish.

Tip: Serve with 2 lemons cut in half and boiled potatoes.

Perch in Beer Sauce

Flussbarsche im Bierteich

Makes 4 servings:

2 pounds perch fillets
juice of 1 lemon
salt, black pepper
2 onions
5 tablespoons vegetable oil
1 teaspoon brown sugar
1 teaspoon flour
1 cup light beer
1 cup dark beer
3 cloves
2 bay leaves
1 tablespoon white wine vinegar

1. Rinse perch fillets under cold running water and pat dry with paper towels. Drizzle with lemon juice and season with salt and pepper.

2. Peel the onions and cut into thin strips; heat vegetable oil in a pan and sauté onions until transparent. Add sugar and flour and continue sautéing for several minutes, stirring.

3. Add the beer (both kinds), a little at a time, along with the cloves and bay leaves.

4. Place fish in the sauce, cover, and cook about 20 minutes. Remove the fish to a serving platter. Strain the sauce through a sieve, season with white wine vinegar and to taste. Pour over the fish.

Tip: Often served in Berlin with boiled potatoes.

Holstein-Style Schnitzel

Schnitzel à la Holstein

The Borchardt on Gendarmenmarkt is the traditional restaurant in Berlin. Soon after it was established in 1853, it became a meeting place for the political, cultural, art, and intellectual scenes. In its early years, during the Wilhelminian era, it was known as the "Breakfast Place" of the Foreign Office, which was just around the corner on Wilhelmstraße. Theodor Fontane, a Wilhelminian poet, was a regular customer and liked the Borchardt "because the proprietors weren't among those 'stuffy hosts' who thought the public was there for them, and not vice-versa." Another regular was diplomat Friedrich von Holstein, Bismarck's "private secretary," who dined in one of the separate rooms there almost daily. The luxurious "Schnitzel à la Holstein" was created for him. After World War II, during the GDR regime, the Borchardt was a dance hall, a company cafeteria, and even a warehouse, until it closed in the 1970s. After Reunification, the Borchardt was restored and is once again a popular meeting place, where VIPs dine frequently. Even Federal Chancellor Gerhard Schröder stopped by occasionally to order a Holstein-Style Schnitzel.

Makes 4 servings:

4 veal cutlets, about 5 ounces each
salt, black pepper
flour for dredging
3 tablespoons vegetable oil
3 tablespoons butter
4 slices white bread
4 eggs
4 anchovy fillets
2 tablespoons marinated capers
8 halfslices smoked salmon (about 5 ounces)
4 sardines in oil
1 small jar caviar (low-end: lumpfish roe; or high-end: real Russian caviar)
2 tablespoons fresh chopped parsley

1 Lightly pound the veal cutlets, season with salt and pepper, and dredge in flour. Tap to remove loose flour.

2 Heat vegetable oil in a large pan and add the cutlets. Add half the butter and fry the schnitzels for 8 to 10 minutes, turning to cook both sides.

3 Place the finished schnitzels on four preheated plates. Add some butter to the pan and fry the eggs. Meanwhile, toast the bread.

4 Place a fried egg on each schnitzel, with an anchovy, and capers sprinkled on top. Cut the toast diagonally, forming triangles, and spread with the rest of the butter

5 Place smoked salmon and a sardine on each triangle. Add some caviar to each and garnish with parsley. Place two pieces of toast on each plate.

Tip: Serve with fried potatoes and green beans tossed in butter.

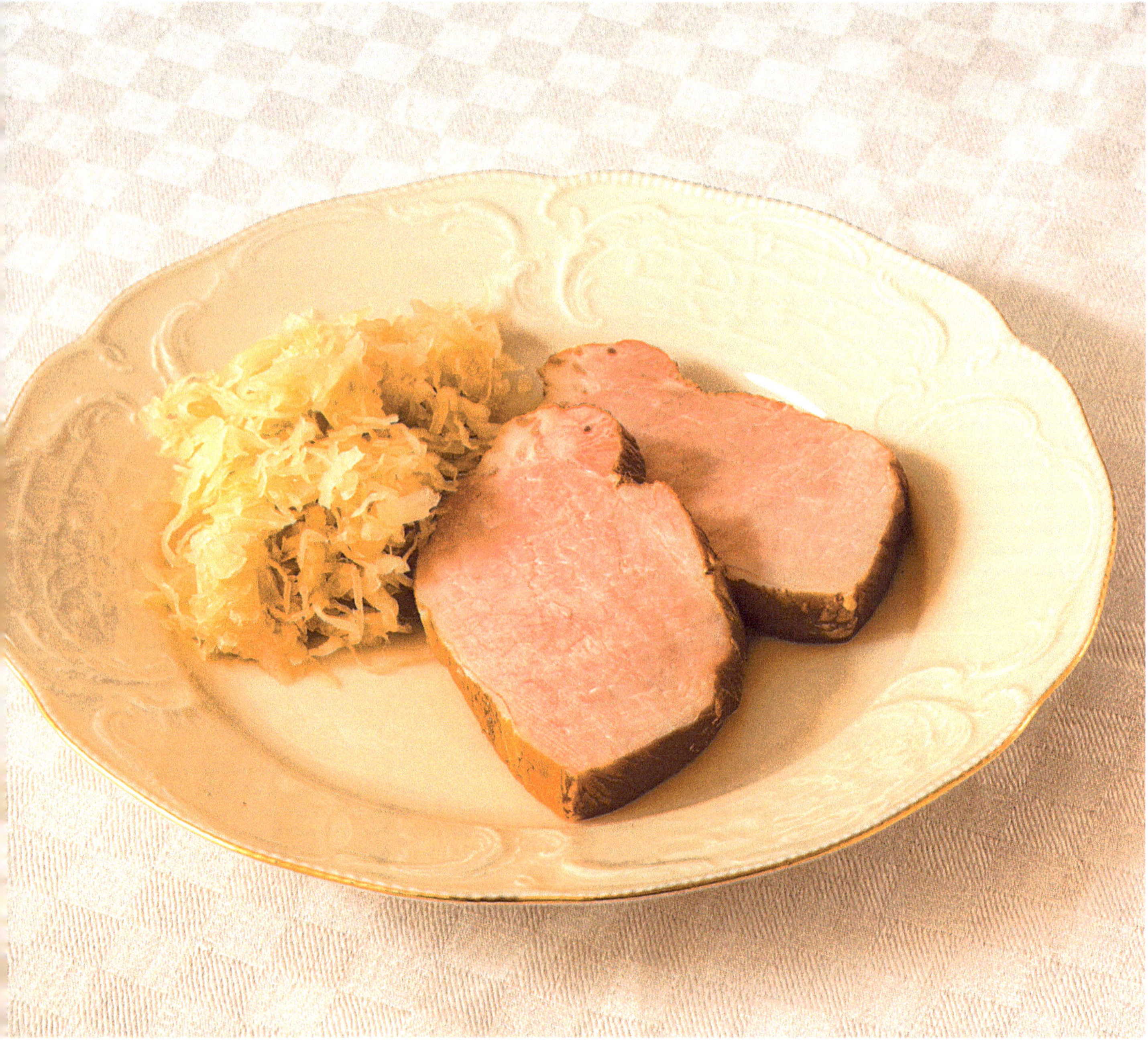

Smoked Pork Loin with Sauerkraut

Kassler auf Sauerkraut

About a hundred years ago in Berlin, a clever master butcher by the name of Johann Cassel came up with the idea of marinating pork loin in a 10 percent salt brine for five days before smoking the meat. Thus Berlin's "Kasseler" (smoked pork loin) was born, and not in the city of Kassel, as many think. In those days—the cured, smoked pork loin was sliced and fried on both sides, in lots of clarified butter, and served with fried potatoes. Many stick the whole thing in the oven and roast it, either browned with a nice crust or encased in a puff pastry, which goes well with red cabbage or mashed potatoes and sauerkraut.

Makes 4 servings:

2 pounds pork loin
5 onions
4 cloves
4 bay leaves
1 carrot
1 apple
2 tablespoons lard
2 pounds sauerkraut
½ cup dry white wine
1 tablespoon black peppercorns
salt
½ cup cream

1 Preheat oven to 390 degrees. Place the pork loin in a roasting pan, with the fatty side facing up.

Peel and chop onion; add onion, cloves, and 2 bay leaves to the pan. Peel and slice the carrot, adding it to the pan as well.

Pour 2 cups boiling water into the pan, and place the pan on the middle rack of the preheated oven. Roast for about 30 minutes, turning the meat two or three times, and adding a little water as needed.

2 Peel the four onions and cut into very slices; braise on all sides in hot lard.

Peel, core, and cut the apple into thin slices; add to the onions. Fluff the sauerkraut with a fork and stir into the onion mixture.

Add white wine to the pot, along with some of the pan drippings from the roaster, and braise the sauerkraut for about 20 minutes. Add the peppercorns and 2 bay leaves. Season with salt to taste.

3 Remove the pork loin from the roasting pan and let stand on a cutting board for several minutes. Strain the pan juices in a sieve and refine with a little cream; season once more to taste. Spoon sauerkraut onto plates. Slice the pork loin and place on the plates with some sauce spooned over the top.

Tip: Earlier, the pork loin broth was mixed with flour to form a creamy gravy; it's easier and tastier to just add cream.

Berliners enjoy munching on leftover pork loin, cold, with mustard or Cumberland sauce. Try this with potato salad.

Pork Knuckle with Broth

Eisbein mit Brühe

If you mention meat, most Berliners will think of pork, and their favorite is "Eisbein," a cured, boiled knuckle of pork. But why is it called "Eisbein"? Way back when, about a hundred years ago, the Spree River was covered in a thick layer of ice. Nothing could get through, and even the barges were frozen in. A mail carrier tied the long bones from a pig to his boots and skated over the ice. His idea wasn't new—skates had long been carved from the strong leg bones of pigs. So it seemed only natural to call a pig's leg "Eisbein" (ice leg). Except in the culinary version, you leave the bone on the plate, after gnawing it clean. Maybe that's what the mail carrier saw when he thought up his skates?

Makes 4 servings:

3 pounds cured pig knuckle, carved into four portions
2 onions
1 bunch soup vegetables (2 carrots, 2 leeks, 2 stalks celery)
2 cloves
2 bay leaves
1 teaspoon black and white peppercorns

1. Wash the meat thoroughly under cold running water, to remove bone splinters. Place in a large pot, cover with cold water, and bring to a boil.

2. Meanwhile, peel and chop the onions. Rinse the vegetables, peel, and chop coarsely. As the water boils in the pot, remove foam with a skimmer.

3. Add the vegetables, cloves, bay leaves, and peppercorns. Cover the pot and cook over medium heat for about 1½ hours.

4. Remove the pork slices from the pot and place them in shallow bowls. Spoon broth over the meat.

Tip: Goes well with puréed peas and sauerkraut. Along with a schnapps and a beer, of course.

Variation:

Degreased Pork-Knuckle Casserole

Remove the freshly boiled meat from the bones and cut into small pieces, trimming away the fat.

Fill the bottom of a casserole dish with a thick layer of sauerkraut. Spread the meat on top and cover with a thick layer of mashed potatoes. Drizzle melted butter over the top, and place the casserole on the middle rack of an oven preheated to 390 degrees; bake about 30 minutes. Serve garnished with browned onion rings. The author enjoys this version of Berliner "Eisbein"; not everyone is a fan of all the fat in the original recipe.

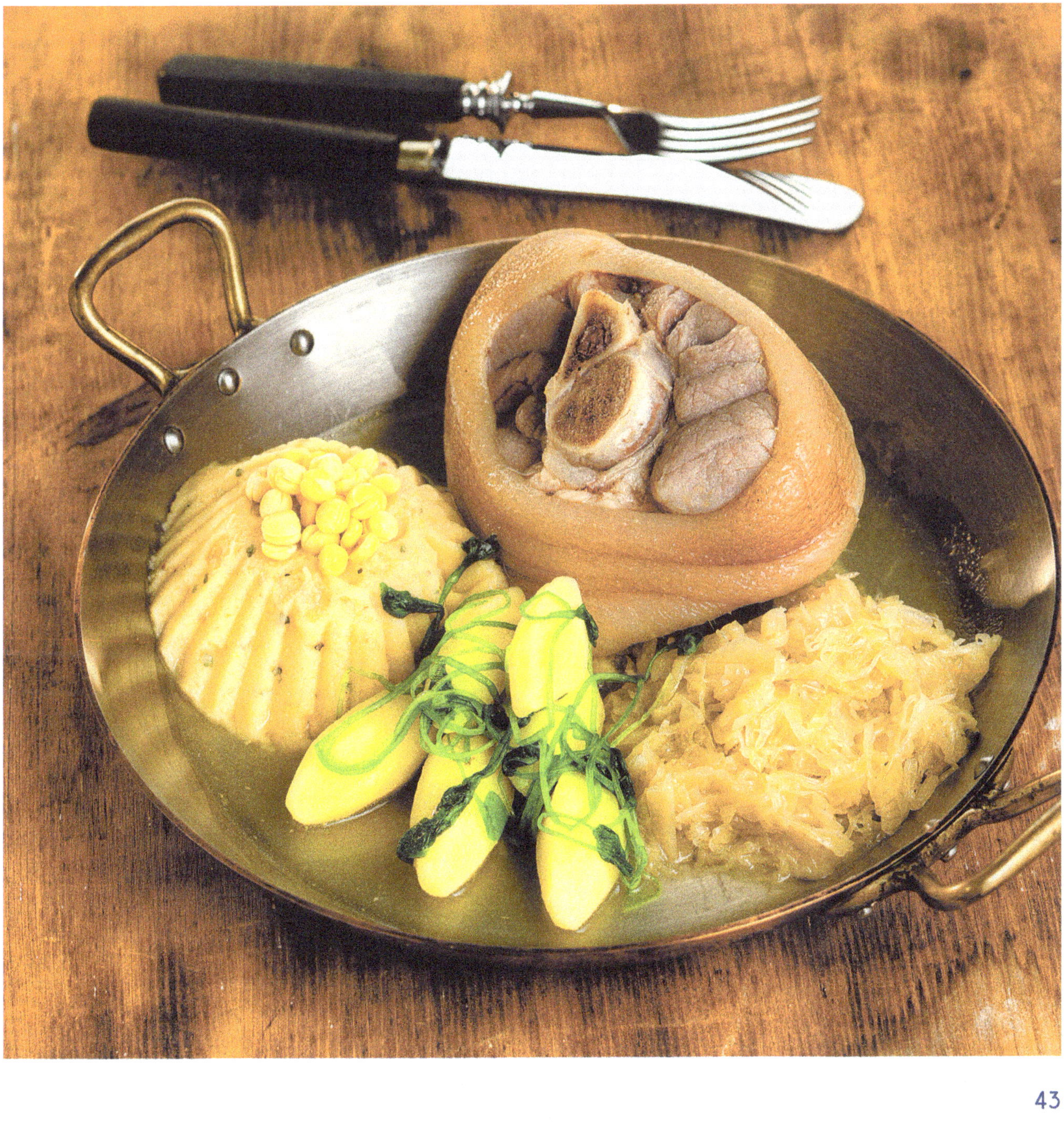

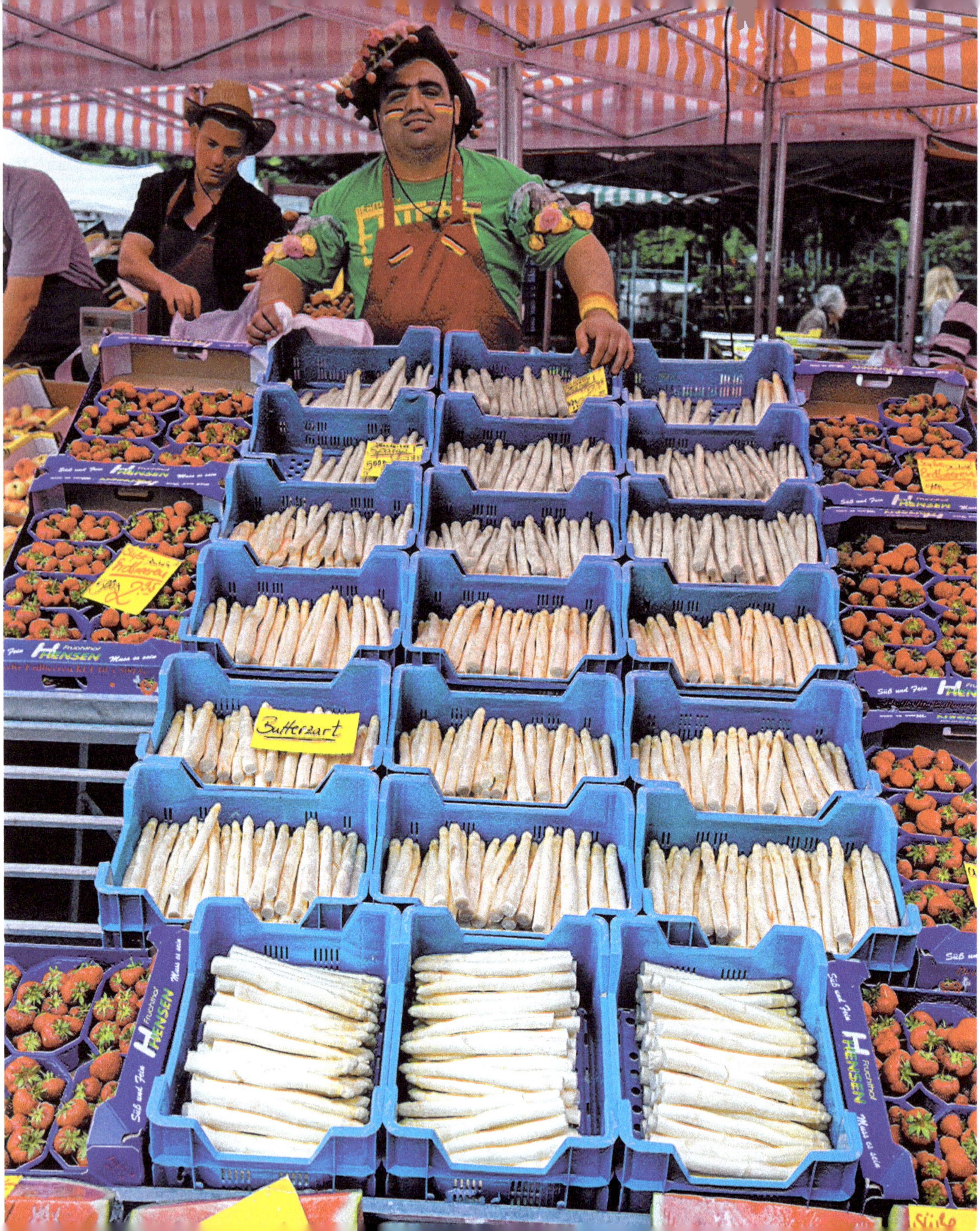
Butterzart

Veal Cakes

Kalbsbrisoletten

The costly veal in this "elegant meatball" increases its stature. The dish came to Berlin with the Huguenots, though veal alone would be too lean—so the Berlin version adds some pork.

A good side dish for veal cakes are chanterelles, a tasty mushroom that can be found in the forests around Berlin. Clean and rinse the chanterelles briefly, pat them dry with a towel, and braise them in a greased pan, also briefly, together with onion rings. Season with salt, pepper, and parsley.

Makes 4 servings:

- 2 shallots
- 2 tablespoons butter
- 1 pound ground veal (pre-order from butcher)
- ½ pound ground pork
- 3 tablespoons grated white bread
- 6 tablespoons milk
- 1 egg
- grated lemon zest from ½ lemon
- 1 tablespoon fresh chopped, mixed herbs
- salt, black pepper
- 2 calves' or pigs' cauls (order from butcher)
- 4 tablespoons vegetable oil

1. Peel and dice shallots and sauté in 1 tablespoon butter until transparent. Place in a bowl with both kinds of ground meat.

2. Mix bread with milk; add this and egg, lemon zest, and herbs to the bowl. Knead well, season with salt and pepper, and form eight flattened meat cakes.

3. Carefully detangle the cauls and place on a cutting board. Cut into eight pieces; wrap one around each meat cake.

4. Heat vegetable oil and the rest of the butter in a large pan; fry the meat cakes for 12 to 15 minutes, turning to cook both sides, until brown and crispy.

Tip: Serve with mashed potatoes, peas, and carrots.

"Faux Rabbit" Meatloaf

"Falscher Hase"

"Falscher Hase" is a dish made with ground meat and softened bread rolls—a clever deception in lean times, when Berliners longed for a nice "Hasenbraten" (roast hare, or actually, rabbit) but could only manage to borrow the name. The dish is actually based on a giant "Bulette" (meatball) shaped like a rabbit, with a hard-boiled egg in the middle, where the rabbit's heart would be.

Makes 4 servings:

2 day-old bread rolls
2 onions
¼ pound bacon
1 teaspoon butter
2 pounds mixed ground meat (beef and pork)
2 eggs
½ teaspoon marjoram
salt, black pepper
1 generous dash each of ground red pepper and ground paprika
1 teaspoon hot mustard
1 tablespoon clarified butter
1 cup hot broth
½ pound spring carrots
1 cup cream
1 tablespoon fresh, chopped parsley

1. Chop the bread rolls and add 1 cup cold water. Peel and mince the onions; dice the bacon.

2. In a pan, render the bacon down and pour over the ground meat. Melt some butter in the pan and sauté the diced onion until transparent. Add to the meat.

3. Knead together with the softened bread and eggs. Season with marjoram, salt, pepper, paprika, and red pepper. Form the meat mixture into an oval "body."

4. Preheat oven to 390 degrees. Heat clarified butter in a roasting pan and place the meatloaf in the pan. Brown meat well on all sides.

5. Place the roasting pan on the middle rack of the preheated oven. Cook for 50 minutes, basting the meat several times with the pan drippings.

6. When the meat is almost done, remove from the oven; clean the carrots and arrange them around the "faux rabbit," return to the oven to cook briefly. Remove the roasting pan from the oven, and carefully remove the meat and carrots from the pan. Bring the pan juices to a brief boil, strain through a sieve, heat again, season to taste and refine with cream.

7. Cut the meatloaf in thick slices and serve with the carrots. Pour the gravy over the plate and garnish with parsley.

Tip: Serve with creamed potatoes and red cabbage or rutabagas and mashed potatoes.

Königsberg Meatballs

Klopse aus Königsberg

Makes 4 servings:

- 1 day-old hard roll
- 5 filleted anchovies
- 1 onion
- 1 pound mixed ground beef and pork
- 1 egg, black pepper
- 1 pinch fresh grated nutmeg
- 2 tablespoons butter
- 1 tablespoon flour
- 1 cup dry white wine
- 2 tablespoons marinated capers
- salt
- 1 teaspoon fresh lemon juice
- 1 quart cream
- 1 egg yolk
- 1 pinch dried marjoram

1 Pour a cup of lukewarm water over the roll. Rinse the anchovies under cold running water, pat dry with a paper towel, and mince. Peel and dice the onion.

2 Knead the ground meat with the softened bread, anchovies, onion, and egg. Season the meat mixture with pepper and nutmeg; let stand.

3 Form walnut-sized meatballs and place them in boiling, salted water. Add the bay leaves and cook about 20 minutes.

4 Stir butter and flour into a white roux, stir in white wine, and add about 4 cups of the meatball broth. Stir thoroughly and garnish with capers. Place the meatballs in the sauce.

5 Stir the lemon juice, salt, and cream into the sauce. Right before serving, whisk the egg yolk in a cup of sauce and return to the pan. Season with marjoram.

Tip: Serve with boiled or mashed potatoes.

"Da Berliner hat es mit de Klopse" (Berliners have a thing for meatballs)—they love these meatballs, in a stew, as a main dish, or as a snack at the pub. As long as they're filling. Königsberg meatballs were originally the national dish of East Prussia, but they're popular in Berlin, too.

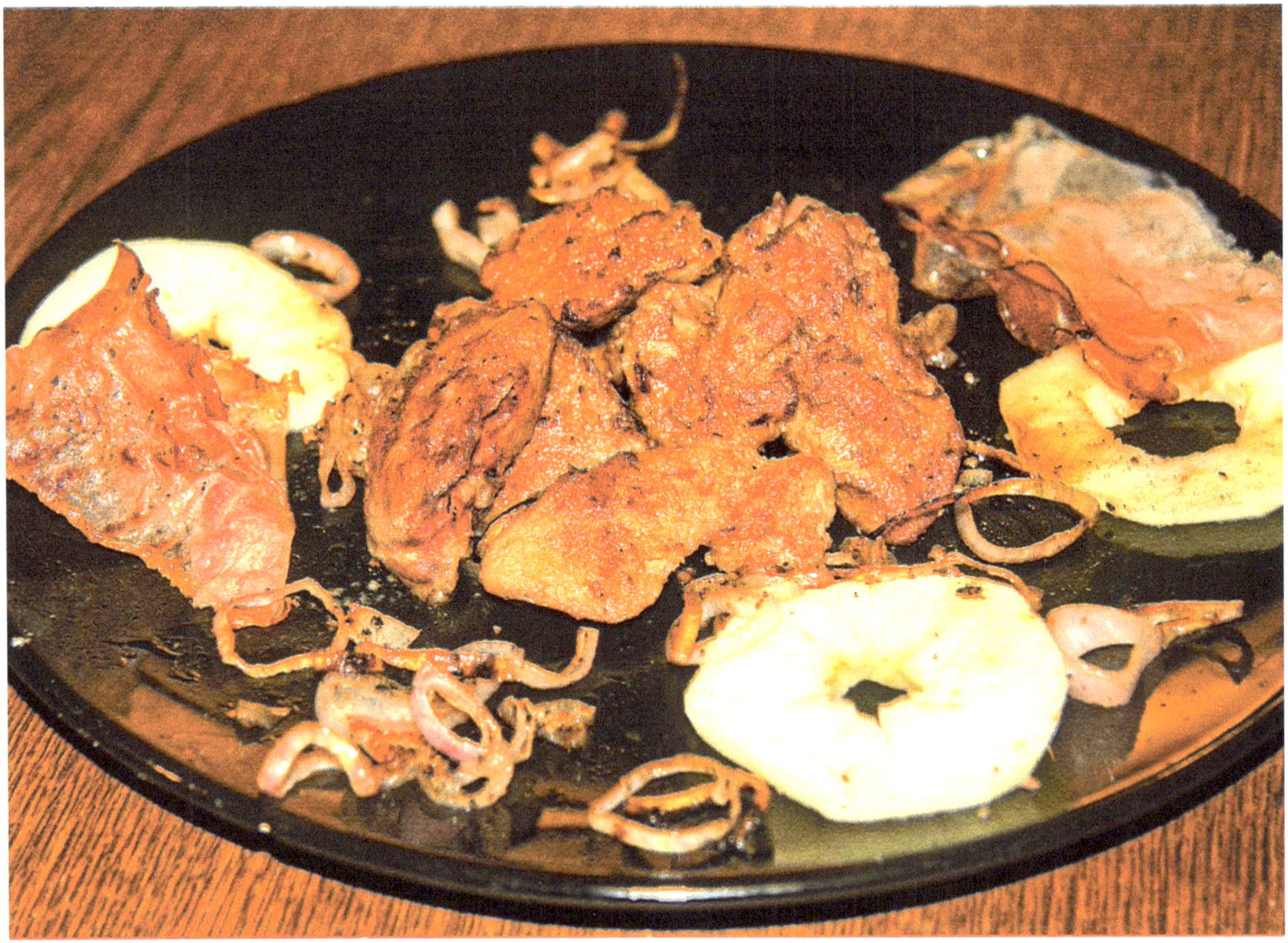

Pan-Fried Berliner Liver

Berliner Leber aus der Pfanne

Berliners like liver. Pork liver is often served, which is less expensive than calves' liver, though the latter tastes better. Chicken livers are used, too. Ask a Berliner in a pub what his liver has to say about all that beer, and he might reply, "Die Leber hat bei uns in Berlin jarnüscht (gar nichts) zu sagen, die machen wir platt in der Pfanne..." (In Berlin, our livers don't have a say; we flatten them...)

Makes 4 servings:

4 slices pork or calves' liver, about ¼ pound each
black pepper
2 tablespoons flour
2 large onions
2 apples (e.g., Boskop, Braeburn, Granny Smith)
2 tablespoons vegetable oil
3 tablespoons butter
8 thin slices bacon
salt

1. Rinse the liver under cold running water and pat dry with paper towels. Season with pepper (the salt comes later, or the liver will harden); dredge in flour, tapping to remove extra flour.

2. Peel the onions and slice into very thin rings. Peel, core, and slice the apples.

3. Heat 1 tablespoon vegetable oil and 1 tablespoon butter in a pan; add the onion and sauté until transparent. Meanwhile, fry the bacon in another pan (no oil needed). Remove from pan and place on paper towels.

4. Heat the rest of the vegetable oil and 1 tablespoon butter in that same pan; place the liver in the pan and fry about 5 minutes, turning to cook both sides; remove from pan, place on a plate, and set aside.

5. Remove the onions from their pan; add the rest of the butter to the pan, and fry the apple slices on both sides.

6. Lightly salt the liver and place on preheated plates. Garnish each with onions and two strips of bacon. Arrange the apple slices on top.

Tip: Mashed potatoes are a must with this dish. Try with tossed salad, if you like; the beverage, in any case, should be beer.

Proud Henry's Thick Bratwursts

Dicke Bratwürste "Stolzer Heinrich"

Thick bratwursts are super fat and boiled in beer. And they taste good—like Bolle! Bolle was the first chain of supermarkets in Berlin, founded in the 19th century by Carl Andreas Julius Bolle. At the time, supermarkets were shops for the upper crust. Those who could afford to shop at Bolle's were doing pretty well. And those who were happy had probably gotten something good from Bolle's. Not to be confused with the popular song about the Berliner Bolle, who went to an amusement park in Pankow where he lost his kid, got beaten up, stabbed, and didn't get any food. The refrain, however, is: "Aber trotzdem hat sich Bolle janz köstlich amüsiert" (but anyway, Bolle had a lot of fun). It is meant to satirize the ever-resilient Berliner.

4 raw brats, about ¼ pound each
1 large onion
¼ pound bacon
4 tablespoons margarine
2 cups light beer
2 bay leaves
5 black peppercorns
1 tablespoon cornstarch
Salt, black pepper

1 Pierce the brats several times with a fork and pour boiling water over them. Pat dry with paper towels.

2 Peel and slice the onion. Dice the bacon and render it down in a hot, greaseless pan; remove to a plate.

3 Heat the margarine in the pan and sauté the onion until transparent. Place the brats in the pan and brown on all sides. Pour the beer into the pan; add the bay leaves and peppercorns and boil about 10 minutes over medium heat.

4 Remove the brats from the pan and place on plates. Continue cooking the beer-brat-onion liquid and add cornstarch (mix starch with 2 tablespoons cold water until smooth, then stir into the pan). Remove the bay leaves, and season the gravy with salt and pepper. Spoon over the brats.

Tip: Serve with mashed potatoes. The original recipe calls for light beer, but dark beer works just fine.

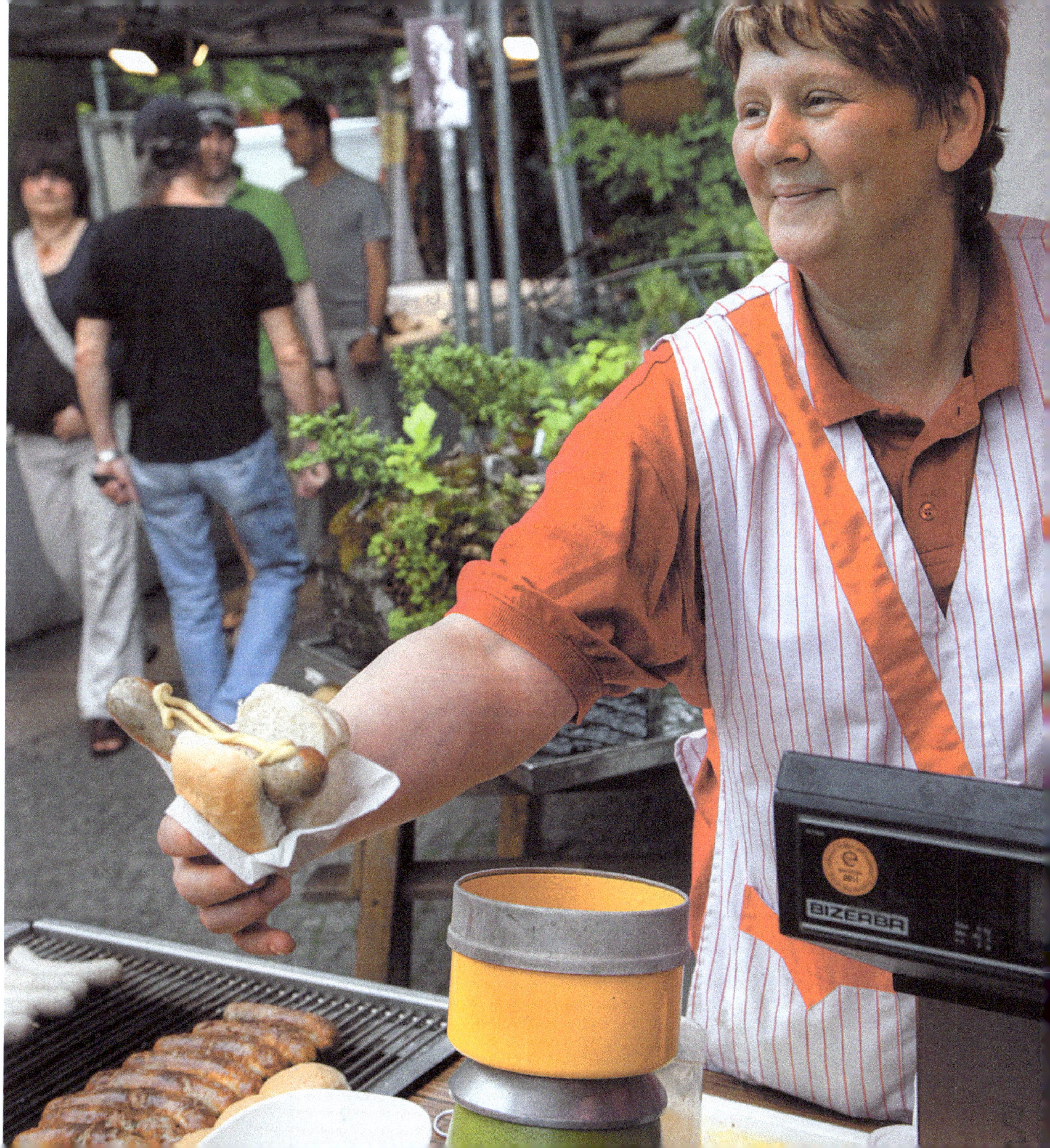
BIZERBA

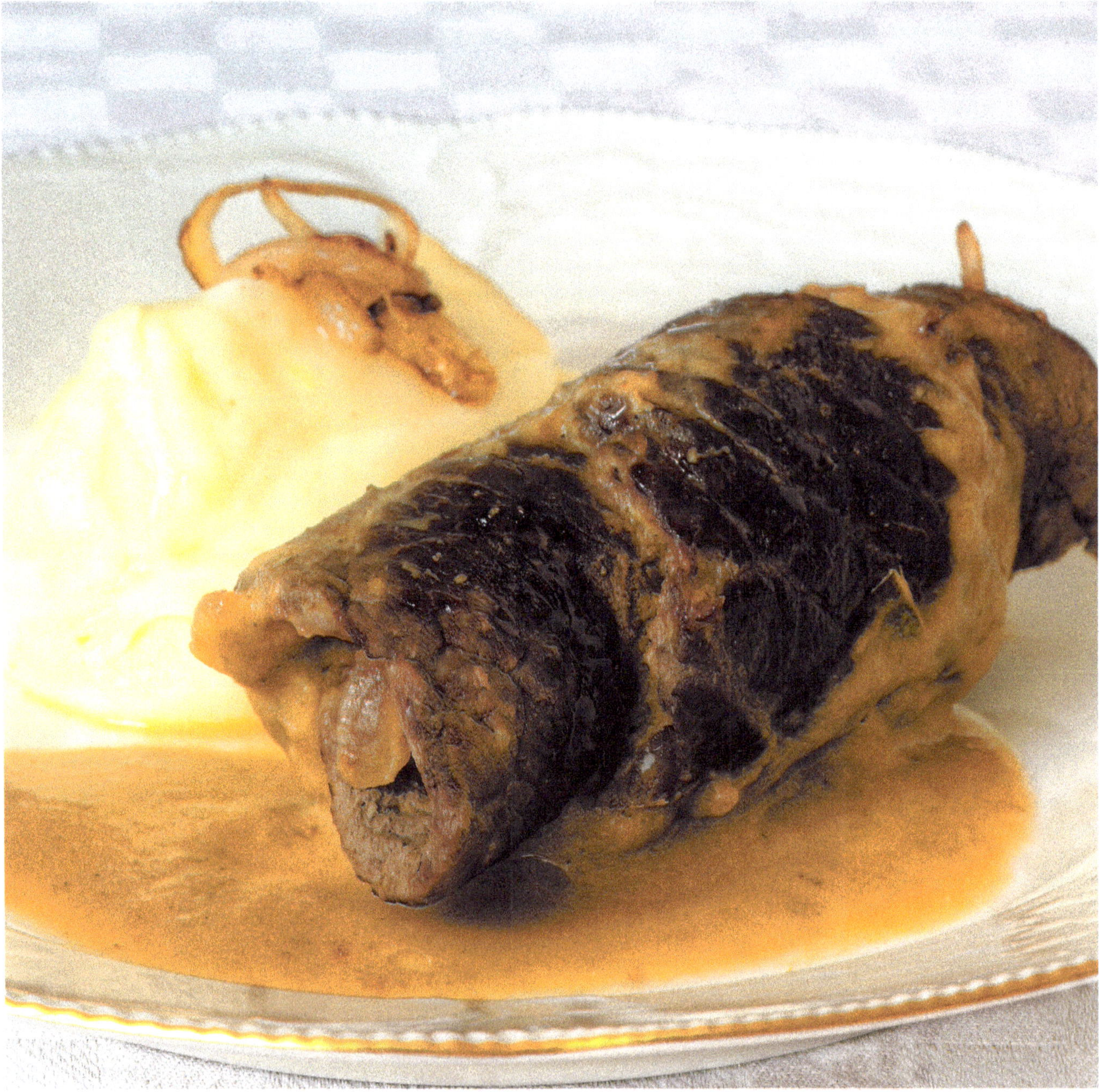

Mother Gerlinde's Beef Roulades

Rinderrouladen von "Mutter Gerlinde"

"*M*olle" (beer) can be found at saloons, bars, und the little pub around the corner, usually covered in beer advertisements. These little beer islands often hang signs in the window, advertising "Futtern wie bei Muttern" (homecooking just like mom's). For some, that might be a deterrent (depending on your mother's culinary abilities), but Mother Gerlinde was a good cook.

4 slices beef roulade (round or rump roast), about ½ pound each
salt, black pepper
1 tablespoon hot mustard
4 thin slices bacon
1 large onion
1 large dill pickle and 2 tablespoons pickle juice
½ bunch soup vegetables (1 carrot, 1 leek, 1 stalk celery)
1 tomato
4 tablespoons vegetable oil
2 bay leaves
1 cup red wine
1 cup meat stock
4 bay leaves
several black peppercorns
1 cup cream

Other: **4 roulade pins**

1. Season both sides of meat with salt and pepper, and place on a work surface. Spread mustard on meat and add a strip of bacon.

2. Peel, halve, and slice the onion into thin strips. Cut the pickle lengthwise, into long strips. Place half the onion and pickle on the meat, roll the meat (with the onion and pickle inside), and secure with roulade pins.

3. Wash the vegetables, peel those that require it, and chop coarsely. Wash and quarter the tomato.

4. Heat the vegetable oil in a wide pot, and braise the roulades on all sides. Add the remaining onion strips, the vegetables, and the tomato quarters to the pan and braise with the meat.

5. Add red wine and broth, peppercorns, bay leaves, and pickle juice.

6. Cover the pot with a lid, and cook the roulades over medium heat about 1¼ hours, turning now and then and adding water as necessary.

7. Remove the roulades from the pot and place on a plate, covered with aluminum foil. Strain the sauce through a sieve and reheat to a boil. Refine with cream and season to taste.

8. Stir any remaining juices from the roulades into the sauce. Serve the roulades with sauce, on preheated plates.

Tip: Good with mixed vegetables and mashed potatoes.

"Dönhoffplatz" Roast Goose

Gänsebraten "Dönhoffplatz"

"*Eene jut jebratene Jans is ne jute Jabe Jottes*" (A well roasted goose is a gift from God), is a favorite saying in Berlin. Especially on holidays, the "Christmas bird" is a must. Kale or red cabbage and potato dumplings usually go along with it. In the early 19th century, there was a goose market on Dönhoffplatz (in the Mitte district) twice a week during Advent. Not only were there Sunday geese there, but goose down, too, for feather beds. The market women were known to be clever and tough, as the following story shows, from a young man who wanted to haggle over the price of a goose:

"Ma'am, Goosey-Loosey has such a sad look on his face, he must be mourning his bride!"
"You little whippersnapper! What do you know of brides, you monkey hatchling?"
"And what's the goose cost, Ma'am?"
"One dollar five,"
"No, it's much too skinny for that."
"Skinny? You think this swamp hog is thin? I'll show you skinny, Sonny. Come here and I'll grab you by the bones till I get calluses on my fingers, and you'll squawk so loud they'll hear you all the way over in Potsdam!"

["*Madamken, der Jänserich hat so n trübes Jesicht, der trauert wohl um seine Braut!*"
"*Du Jrinschnabel, du! Wat weeßt du ausjebrütetes Affenküken von ne Braut!*"
"*Und wat kost de Jans, Madamken?*"
"*Enen Dahler, fünf Jute!*"
"*Nee, davor is se zu mager!*"
"*Wat, mager soll diese Oderbruchsche sein? Du bist mager, mein Söhneken, komm mal her, ick werde dir an deine Knochen fassen, det ick Schwielen an de Finger krieje, und du quietschst, det man s noch in Potsdam hören soll!*"]

Makes 4 large servings or more!

1 prepared goose, approx. 8 pounds, traditionally from Poland
salt, black pepper
1 bunch mugwort
5 tart apples (e.g., Boskop, Braeburn, or Granny Smith)
2 onions
1 tablespoon cornstarch

1 Rinse the goose under cold running water, washing thoroughly and removing fat from inside the abdominal cavity. Pat dry with paper towels; season inside and out with salt and pepper.

2 Preheat oven to 350 degrees. Wash the mugwort and shake dry. Wash, core, and cut apples into quarters; do not peel.

3 Put apples and mugwort inside abdominal cavity. Sew shut with cooking thread and bind the legs together.

4 Place goose in roasting pan, breast-side up; pour 1 cup water around side of pan. Place pan on lowest rack in preheated oven. Roast goose about 2½ hours.

5 Midway through the roasting time, poke a needle into the goose, beneath the leg, to allow fat to run out. Peel and slice onions and spread them around the pan—they'll taste good and soak up fat. Pour an additional 2 cups cold water around the side.

6 Increase oven temperature by 40 degrees, or turn to the "grill" setting, to brown the

goose in about 20 minutes. Remove the goose from the roasting pan and place it back in the oven on aluminum foil, with the oven turned off.

7 Place the roasting pan on the stove. Add 2 cups hot water and bring the pan drippings to a boil. Strain through a fine sieve and bring to a boil again. Mix cornstarch with 3 tablespoons cold water, until smooth, and add to the gravy. Season to taste with salt and pepper.

8 Remove the thread and cut the goose in half. Arrange the apples on a preheated serving platter. Cut the legs and wings from the halves. Cut the halves into smaller portions and arrange on a large serving platter. Serve with the gravy.

Thick Egg Noodles with Bureaucrat's Sauce

Dicke Eiernudeln mit Beamtenstippe

Probably the only traditional dish in Berlin that doesn't include potatoes, turnips, or cabbage, but is served with noodles instead, though maybe only because frugal households stretch their beloved "Hackepeter" (seasoned raw meatloaf) with lots of gravy. And potatoes don't go well with this particular gravy anyway. Today, of course, noodles are more common in Berlin, thanks to many Italian immigrants' restaurants.

Makes 4 servings:

1 pound egg noodles of your choice
½ pound prepared "Hackepeter" (seasoned raw meatloaf with onions, from the butcher)
3 tablespoons vegetable oil
1 tablespoon tomato paste
1 teaspoon marjoram
salt, black pepper
1 cup meat stock

1. Cook the noodles in boiling, lightly salted water about 10 minutes, until al dente.

2. Meanwhile, brown the Hackepeter in hot vegetable oil until crumbly; add tomato paste and heat briefly. Season with marjoram, salt, and pepper (carefully), and add meat stock.

3. Cook 10 minutes over low heat, stirring. Strain the noodles in a colander and serve in shallow bowls. Spoon the bureaucrat's sauce over the noodles.

Leftover Hash

Hoppelpoppel – Happen-Pappen

A delicious dish to make with leftovers, but you can also use fresh ingredients. This skillet meal contains meat, onions, potatoes, and eggs. Berliners can be really hungry when they dig into this dish—so just put the pan on the table and give everyone a fork.

Makes 4 large servings:

- 1 large onion
- 1 pound leftover fried or boiled meat
- 4 tablespoons margarine
- 1 pound boiled potatoes (skin on), sliced
- salt, black pepper
- 4 eggs

1. Peel, halve, and dice the onions. Cut up the leftover meat.

2. Heat 2 tablespoons margarine in each of two pans. Place the onion and leftover meat in one pan, and the onion and potatoes in the other.

3. Season the contents of each pan with salt and pepper, and fry until crispy.

4. When the potatoes are golden brown, transfer them to the meat pan—carefully, so the potatoes aren't squashed.

5. Whisk the eggs and pour over the meat/potato mixture, cook briefly, and place the pan on the table. Guten Appetit!

Tip: In Berlin "Hoppelpoppel" is also the name of a drink: beat 4 egg yolks with 3 tablespoons sugar and 1 cup cream in a heat-proof bowl, over a hot water bath (double boiler), until creamy. Pour into punch glasses and dust with ground nutmeg.

Rutabaga Stew

Steckrübeneintopf

In lean times, of which there have been many in Berlin, tables weren't decked with Sunday roasts, but with watery stews. The rutabaga, a robust and reasonably priced vegetable, was synonymous with wartime hunger. Berliners still enjoy stews today, along with a good dose of gratitude and hope that the bad times are all behind them—and a little bacon...

Makes 4 servings:

1 rutabaga, about 4 cups chopped
½ bunch soup vegetables (1 carrot, 1 leek, 1 stalk celery)
1 small onion
1 bunch parsley
¼ pound smoked bacon
2 tablespoons vegetable oil
salt
fresh ground pepper
2 cups meat stock
½ cup sour cream

1. Rinse, peel, and chop the rutabaga. Rinse the soup vegetables, peel the carrot, and chop all. Peel and dice the onion. Rinse the parsley and pat dry; remove stems and mince the leaves. Dice the bacon.

2. Heat the vegetable oil in a pot; add the bacon and onion, and braise. Stir in the vegetables, a little at a time, and braise for several minutes. Season with salt and pepper. Add the stock to the pot, bring to a boil, and simmer over medium heat for about 20 minutes.

3. Season the stew to taste and serve in soup bowls; garnish with sour cream and plenty of parsley.

Tip: Serve with rolls.

Pea Soup with Ears and Snouts

Löffelerbsen mit Ohren und Schnauzen

This dish is named for the famous "Berliner Schnauze" (snout), that endearing bluntness with which Berliners say exactly what's on their minds, without mincing any words. They don't usually mean for things to sound as harsh as they do.

Tip: Goes well with hard rolls.

Makes 4 servings:

1 pound hulled, yellow peas
1 bacon rind
½ pound pickled pig ears
½ pound pickled pig snout
4 fresh sprigs marjoram
1 onion
1 carrot
1 parsley root
1 leek
1 pound potatoes
salt, black pepper
1 tablespoon fresh chopped parsley

1 Cover the peas in cold water and soak in a pot for at least 8 hours. Bring the pot to a boil. Stir in the bacon rind, pig ears, pig snout, and marjoram.

2 Peel and dice the onion, carrot, and parsley root. Cut the leek in half lengthwise, rinse between the layers, and cut diagonally in strips.

3 Add the vegetables to the pot and add water, if necessary. Simmer over medium heat for about 2 hours, skimming foam off the surface from time to time.

4 Cut the pig ears in thin strips and remove the meat from the pig snout and cut into small pieces. Peel and dice the potatoes.

5 Add the ears, snout meat, and potatoes to the stew and cook another 20 minutes. Lightly season with salt and pepper. Stir in parsley and serve.

Emperor Wilhelm II's Potato Soup

Kartoffelsuppe "Kaiser Wilhelm II"

Makes 4 to 6 servings:

½ pound celery root
1 carrot
4 Teltow turnips
1 onion
¼ pound cooked ham
1 bunch parsley
2 pounds potatoes
1 tablespoon vegetable oil
1 tablespoon butter
salt, black pepper
1 pinch ground nutmeg
1 bay leaf
2 cups meat stock
1 quart cream
1 egg

1 Rinse, peel, and chop the celery root, carrot, and turnips. Peel and mince the onion. Dice the ham. Rinse the parsley, pat dry, remove stems, and mince the leaves.

2 Peel the potatoes and cut into uniform pieces. Heat vegetable oil and butter in a pot; add onion and ham to the pot and braise. Slowly add the rest of the vegetables and braise. Season with salt, pepper, and nutmeg. Add the bay leaf and meat stock; bring to a boil. Reduce heat and simmer for about 20 minutes. Stir in the cream and puree with a hand mixer until creamy. Whisk the egg in a cup of soup and return to the pot. Season to taste and serve hot. Garnish generously with parsley.

Aunt Hannelore's Lentil Stew

Linsensuppe von Tante Hannelore

Makes 4 servings:

¼ pound smoked bacon
1 onion
½ bunch soup vegetables (1 carrot, 1 leek, 1 stalk celery)
2 Teltow turnips
2 tablespoons vegetable oil
1 cup lentils
4 ounces red wine or Berliner beer
2 bay leaves
1 sprig thyme
1 pound pork loin (bone-in)
salt, black pepper
2 ounces sour cream

1. Dice the bacon. Peel and mince the onion. Rinse and finely chop the soup vegetables and the turnips.

2. Heat the vegetable oil in a pot and braise the bacon and onion. Add the vegetables to the pot and braise several minutes. Stir in the lentils and braise everything together for several more minutes.

3. Stir in red wine and two pints warm water. Add bay leaves, sprig of thyme, and pork loin, and cook about 50 minutes over medium heat.

4. Remove the pork loin from the pot, remove the meat from the bones, and cut into bite-sized pieces. Season the stew with salt and pepper and refine with sour cream.

5. Place the pork pieces in deep, preheated soup plates and spoon the thick soup over the meat.

*B*erliners eat all kinds of cabbage—red cabbage, kale, sauerkraut, and savoy. That's because a great deal of cabbage is grown all around Berlin, and it's inexpensive and easy to store. This recipe calls for white or savoy cabbage.

Grandpa Lothar's Stuffed Cabbage Leaves

Kohlrouladen nach Opa Lothar

Makes 4 servings:

8 large cabbage leaves
salt
1 day-old bread roll
½ cup hot milk
1 onion
1 clove garlic
¼ pound cooked ham
2 tablespoons butter
1 pound mixed ground meat (ground beef and pork)
1 egg
salt, black pepper
zest from ½ lemon
1 teaspoon dried thyme
1 tablespoon fresh, chopped herbs (parsley, chervil)
½ bunch soup vegetables (1 carrot, 1 leek, 1 stalk celery)
4 tablespoons vegetable oil
2 cups hot meat stock
½ cup crème fraîche
Other: **kitchen thread**

1. Wash the cabbage leaves and blanch 1 minute in boiling water. Drain, rinse in cold water, and strain. Pour hot milk on the bread roll and cover with a cloth.

2. Peel and mince the onion and garlic. Dice the ham. Sauté in ½ tablespoon butter with the onion and garlic, until the onion is transparent.

3. In a large bowl, combine the contents of the pan, the egg, and the softened bread with the ground meat and knead until thoroughly mixed. Season with salt, pepper, lemon peel, thyme, and herbs.

4. Place the savoy leaves on a cutting board and cut off the thick ribs. Place some of the meat mixture in the middle of each leaf, fold the leaves around the contents, and wrap securely with the kitchen thread.

5. Preheat the oven to 390 degrees. Rinse the soup vegetables and cut into small pieces.

6. Heat the vegetable oil and the remaining butter in a roasting pan, and braise the stuffed cabbage rolls on all sides. Add the vegetables and braise. Pour in the meat stock, bring to a boil, and place the lid on the roasting pan.

7. Place the roasting pan on the middle rack in the preheated oven and braise the stuffed cabbage rolls about 1¼ hours. Remove the stuffed cabbage and place on a preheated serving platter.

8. Strain the sauce, bring to a boil, and refine with crème fraîche.

Tip: Sauces used to be thickened with starch. Today, old recipes are updated with cream or crème fraîche instead.

Not-So-Elegant Chicken Fricassee

Nicht so vornehmes Hühnerfrikassee

The Adlon is a luxury hotel on Pariser Platz, right across from the Brandenburg Gate, next to the American embassy. The original hotel was founded by Lorenz Adlon in 1907. Before World War II, prominent figures stayed here: Charlie Chaplin, Josephine Baker, and Marlene Dietrich. Films like Grand Hotel with Greta Garbo, and Billy Wilder's comedy One, Two, Three were filmed here. After the Berlin Wall was built, the war-damaged hotel was suddenly in no-man's land, and it was torn down in 1984. It was rebuilt in the 1990s and reopened in 1997. Today, prominent figures abound once more, from the late Michael Jackson to Barack Obama. The Adlon serves a rather elegant, extravagant chicken fricassee, made of veal tongue, crayfish tails, black morels, sweetbread, and asparagus, recommended for professional cooks only. Here's a variation for the common household.

Makes 4 servings:

1 prepared chicken, approx. 3 pounds
salt
½ bunch soup vegetables (1 carrot, 1 leek, 1 stalk celery)
2 tablespoons butter
1 tablespoon flour
1 cup cream
white pepper
1 egg yolk
½ pound mushrooms
½ pound frozen peas
a dash of lemon juice

Garnish with:

4 shelled crayfish tails
¼ pound asparagus tips from a jar
1 tablespoon fresh chervil leaves

1 Rinse the chicken under cold running water, inside and out. Place in a pot, pour in cold water, and bring the water to a boil. When the water boils, pour off the water, replace it with fresh, cold water. Bring the new water to a boil. Add salt.

2 Clean the soup vegetables, cut into small pieces, and place in the pot. Cook the chicken over medium heat for about 1½ hours.

3 Remove the cooked chicken from the pot, cut in half, remove the skin and legs. Cut the chicken meat into bite-sized pieces.

4 Strain the chicken broth. In a pan, stir butter and flour to form a blond roux and slowly add the broth.

5 Cook the gravy, stirring, until thick. Refine with cream and season to taste with salt and pepper. Whisk the egg yolk with a ladleful of sauce and return it to the pot, stirring. Remove from heat and let stand.

6 Add the mushrooms and peas to the sauce, followed a few minutes later by the chicken. Season to taste once more, and add a couple dashes of lemon juice.

7 Serve the chicken fricassee on warmed plates and garnish with asparagus tips, arranged around the edges of the plate. Place a crayfish tail in the middle of each serving and garnish with chervil leaves.

Tip: You can also add the garnishes to the fricassee during the last minute of cooking time.

Chapter Three:
"Gimme plenty potatoes, but easy on the veggies"

"Jib man ordentlich Kartoffeln – aber spar mit's Jemüse"

Mashed Potatoes

Quetschkartoffeln

King Friedrich II of Prussia, better known as Friedrich the Great, or "Old Fritz," brought these unfamiliar tubers from America in 1756. In his "Potato Mandate," he instructed all Prussian officials to teach farmers how to grow potatoes, and he had potatoes planted everywhere, even around the Prussian town halls. Many farmers resisted, especially because some had tried to eat them raw. Many dug the potatoes up again, under the cover of night, and planted cabbage instead. Eventually it occurred to the king to place the royal fields under military guard. Only then did some farmers realize that potatoes might be valuable. Once Berliners discovered their taste, they started eating potatoes with everything, and they became the Prussians' favorite meal.

Makes 4 servings:

2 pounds potatoes
salt
1 bay leaf
1 cup lukewarm milk
2 tablespoons butter, at room temperature
1 pinch ground nutmeg

1 Peel potatoes and cut in half (quarters, if large). Cook 30 minutes in lightly salted water with the bay leaf.

2 Mash the potatoes with a potato masher or using a grater. Mix with milk and butter, and season with salt and nutmeg.

Tip: You can still get authentic potato mashers, which coarsely crush the potatoes without turning them to mush.

Potato Purée

Kartoffelpüree

Cook the potatoes until tender and purée using a hand mixer. In a pot on the stove, stir just under 1 cup milk and 2 tablespoons warm butter into the potato purée until creamy and glistening. Season with salt, pepper, and nutmeg.

Berlin Broth Potatoes

Berliner Brühkartoffeln

Makes 4 servings:

½ bunch soup vegetables (1 carrot, 1 leek, 1 stalk celery)
2 pounds potatoes
6 cups meat stock
salt, black pepper
1 pinch ground nutmeg

1 Clean the soup vegetables, peel as necessary, and dice. Peel potatoes and cut into bite-sized pieces.

2 Put the vegetables and potatoes in a pot with the broth and bring to a boil. Reduce the heat and cook until the potatoes are tender, approximately 20 minutes.

3 Season with salt, pepper, and nutmeg, and serve in shallow bowls.

Tip: Serve with sausages, pork loin, or boiled meats.

Potato Pancakes

Kartoffelpuffer

Makes 4 servings:

**2 pounds potatoes
salt
1 onion
1 egg
1-2 tablespoons flour
clarified butter for frying**

1 Wash the potatoes and cook in lightly salted water until tender. Peel potatoes and grate. Peel the onion and grate, too, and combine with the potatoes.

2 Mix the potato mixture with the egg and flour, and knead briefly.

3 Heat plenty of clarified butter in a pan. Place the potato mixture in the pan, one lump at a time, and flatten with a spoon.

4 Fry the potato pancakes on both sides until golden brown and crispy.

Tip: Berliners eat these with applesauce or dust with sugar and eat with coffee. These are not meant to be sweets, however.

Home Fries with Bacon, Onions, and Egg

Bratkartoffeln mit Speck, Zwiebeln und Ei

This is the classical Berlin dish; it even describes a relationship: "Bratkartoffel-Verhältnis". This is when a guy carries on a friendship with a woman for her cooking only without having any intention to committ eventually.

Makes 4 servings:

1 tablespoon vegetable oil or butter
2 pounds of potatoes, steamed and peeled
salt, pepper
4 ounces of bacon or prosciutto
1 egg
1 tablespoon minced chives

1. Slice the potatoes, the onions, and the bacon

2. Heat the oil (or the butter) in a large, nonstick pan.

3. Put the sliced potatoes in the oil, season with salt and pepper.

4. Roast potato slices on both sides for 5 minutes altogether with medium heat.

5. Mix in the thinly sliced onions and the bacon.

6. Keep simmering the pan on lower heat for another 10 minutes, turn the potatoes around frequently.

7. Crack the egg and pour it over the potatoes. Stir, let it thicken for 1 more minute.

8. Decorate the dish with the chives before serving.

Tip: Goes well with Bockwurst, or meatballs, or Kassler. Best results with oven potatoes baked the previous day and kept wrapped in aluminium foil in the fridge. Also: add a little garlic, if you like it.

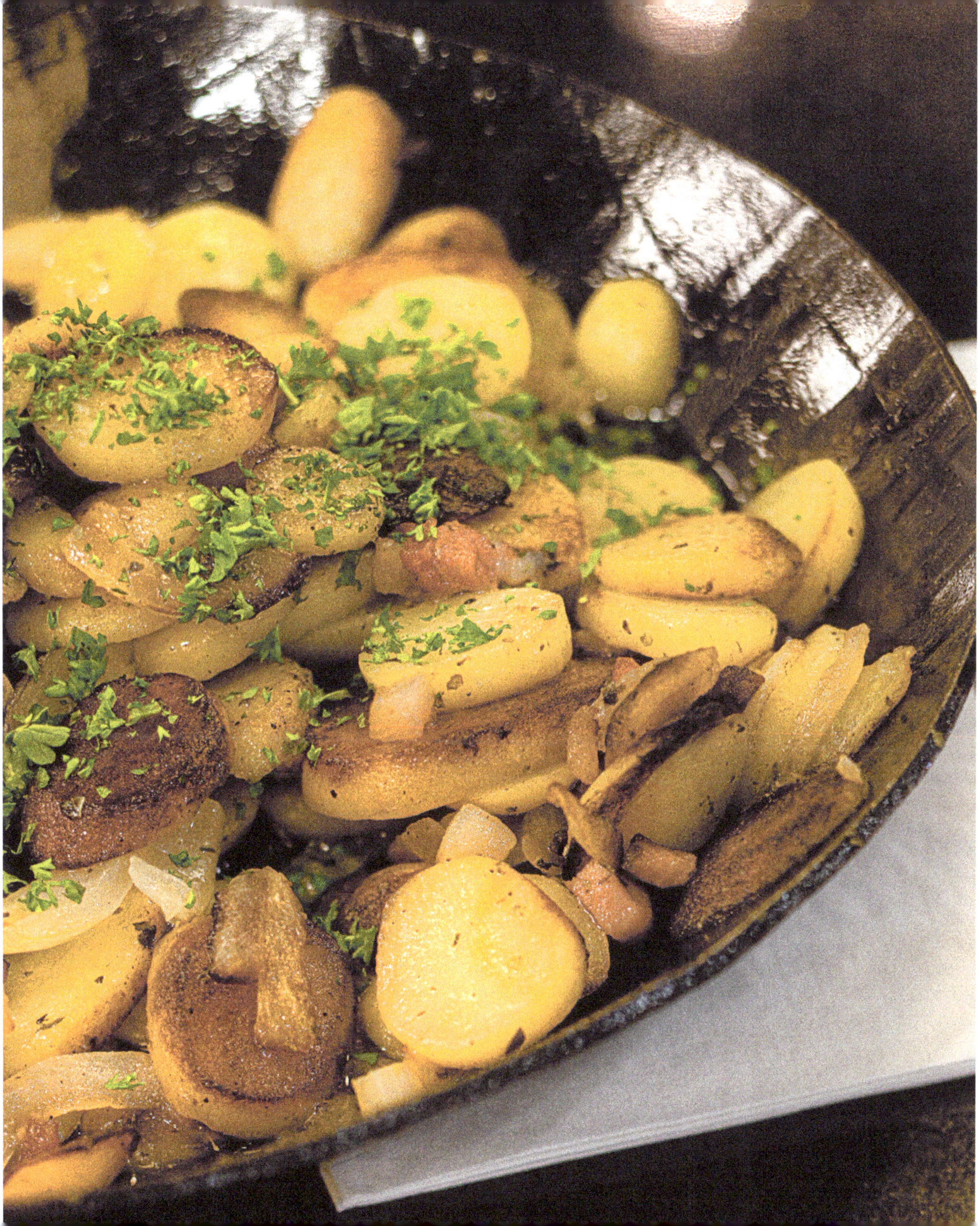

Eggs with Mustard Sauce

Eier mit Mostrichsauce

This is a typical Berlin dish and is still served, for example, in the oldest restaurant in Berlin, "Zur letzten Instanz" (Final Judgment), a traditional restaurant in the Mitte district. Established not far from Alexanderplatz on Waisenstraße in 1621, the building has been completely remodeled and renovated since then. The current name didn't come about until the 1920s, though, when a courthouse was built next door. Citizens fortified themselves at the restaurant before going to court, fighting for their rights, and receiving their "final judgment."

Makes 4 servings:

8 eggs
2 tablespoons butter
1 tablespoon flour
1 tablespoon hot mustard
1 tablespoon sugar
3 tablespoons white wine vinegar
2 cups meat stock
salt, black pepper
1 tablespoon fresh, chopped parsley

1 Place the eggs in boiling water and boil 8 minutes. Meanwhile, heat flour and butter on the stove and stir into a brown roux.

2 Stir in mustard, sugar, white wine vinegar, and broth.

3 Keep stirring vigorously—the gravy that forms should be thick, creamy, and smooth. Rinse the eggs in cold water, peel, and cut in half lengthwise.

4 Place four egg halves on each plate and spoon mustard sauce over the eggs. Sprinkle with parsley.

Tip: Goes well with mashed potatoes and mixed vegetables.

Puréed Peas

Erbspüree

Berliners love this green goo, for what would pork knuckles, pork loins, meat platters, or even eggs with mustard sauce be without puréed peas? Probably left alone. Those who don't like the salty puréed peas from commercial mixes can make this side dish with their own, fresh ingredients.

Makes 4 servings:

- 1 pound dried, yellow peas
- ¼ pound celery root
- 1 carrot
- 1 parsley root
- 1 bacon rind (or a small piece of bacon)
- 2 sprigs each of marjoram and thyme
- ½ bunch parsley
- 1 onion
- ¼ pound bacon
- 1 tablespoon clarified butter
- salt

1. Soak the peas in 2 cups water for at least 8 hours. Using the same water, heat to a boil.

2. Peel and dice the celery root, carrot, and parsley root. Add these and the bacon rind (or bacon) to the peas. Wash the marjoram, thyme, and a few sprigs of parsley, and add to the pot. Cook for about 1½ hours.

3. Shortly before the end of the cooking time, peel and dice the onion. Dice the bacon, too. Rinse the rest of the parsley, pat it dry, remove the leaves from the stem, and mince.

4. Heat the clarified butter; add the diced bacon and onion. Remove the herbs and bacon from the broth in the other pot. Purée the peas, using a hand mixer, and salt lightly. Serve the puréed peas and sprinkle with the bacon and onion.

Teltow Turnips

Teltower Rübchen

These white turnips originated in the small town of Teltow, in Brandenburg, near the gates of Berlin, and were recorded as early as the Middle Ages. Until 1711, the white turnips were raised by just a few Teltow residents, some in private gardens, some in farm fields. The yield of these tasty turnips was so small that they were carried in baskets to Berlin to offer for sale. Even Goethe raved about the taste of these tender turnips.

Makes 4 servings:

2 pounds Teltow turnips
4 tablespoons butter
2 tablespoons sugar
5 ounces (⅝ cup) beef or vegetable broth
salt
freshly ground pepper

1 Wash and lightly scrape the turnips; cut in half (or quarters, if the turnips are large).

2 Heat the butter in a wide pot until frothy; stir in the sugar. When the sugar has dissolved, add the turnips and toss back and forth.

3 Pour in the broth and cook for ½ hour, until tender. Season with salt and pepper.

Tip: Goes well with roasts.

Kale

Grünkohl

Berliners love kale with roast goose, duck, pork loin, or other cured and smoked meats—but don't forget the potatoes, too. It's a winter vegetable and tastes even better after the first frost, which turns the plant's starch into sugar.

Makes 4 servings:

2 pounds kale
salt
2 tablespoons clarified butter or rendered pork (or goose) fat
freshly ground pepper
1 dash sugar
1 cup meat stock

If desired: **1 teaspoon flour**
1 pinch freshly grated nutmeg

1. Wash the kale and cook 10 minutes in lightly salted water. Remove from the pot, shake dry, remove thick ribs, and finely chop the leaves.

2. Heat the butter or lard in a wide pot; add the cabbage, and sauté 10 minutes, seasoning with salt, pepper, and sugar. Add the broth, cover, and cook the cabbage for about 40 minutes.

3. When the kale is tender, dust with flour and stir well. Season again to taste and add nutmeg.

Tip: Try adding ham with the broth, which enhances the flavor.

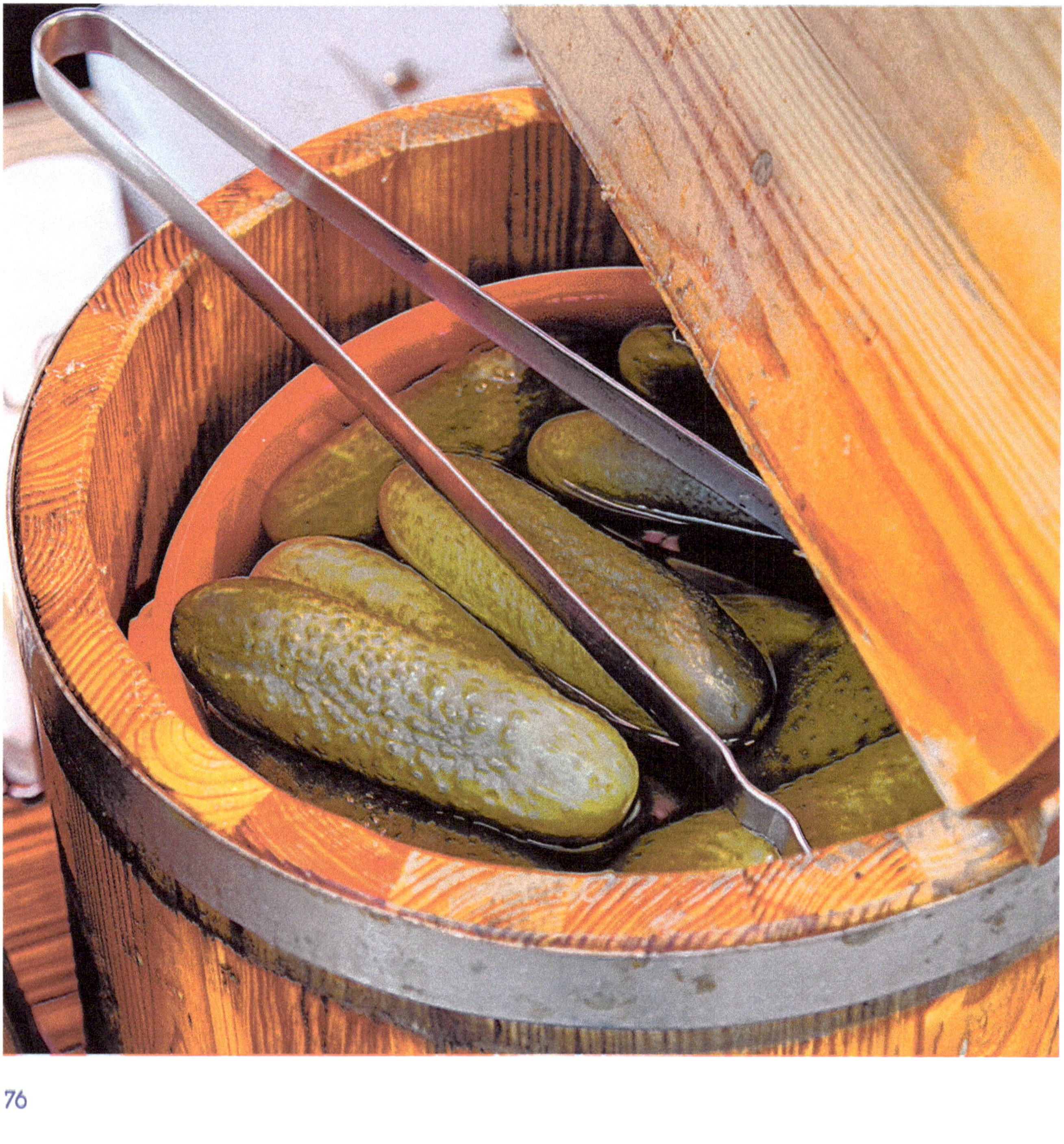

Braised Cucumbers

Schmorgurkengemüse

The Spreewald, southeast of Berlin, has more than eels—it's famous for cucumbers, too. These are processed as dill pickles, mustard pickles, pepper pickles, and garlic pickles, depending on their size. Since the Wall came down, Spreewald cucumbers are available in all sizes and varieties in Berlin markets again.

Makes 4 servings:

2 pounds cucumbers (3 or 4)
1 onion
2 ounces bacon
2 tablespoons vegetable oil
salt, black pepper
1 dash sugar
1 dash white vinegar
½ cup cream
½ bunch fresh, chopped dill

1. Peel the cucumbers, cut lengthwise, and scrape out the seeds with a spoon. Slice each half. Peel and mince the onion. Mince the bacon.

2. Heat the vegetable oil in a wide pot; add the ham and onion, and sauté. Add the cucumbers and braise in their own juice, about 10 minutes, tossing often. Add a little water, if necessary.

3. Season with salt, pepper, sugar, and vinegar. Refine with cream. Stir in the dill right before serving.

Chapter Four: Desserts

The most famous dessert in Berlin is called a "Berliner"—everywhere except in Berlin, where the fried dessert filled with jelly is called "Pfannkuchen" (literally, pancake, though what's meant is actually a jelly donut). What's called a pancake everywhere else is called "Eierkuchen" in Berlin (egg cake). And in Bavaria, jelly donuts are called "Krapfen." Whatever they're called, Berliners are balls of yeast dough deep-fried in hot oil. The filling is very important, which can be jelly, egg liqueur, or chocolate. During Carnival, though, watch out: you might find your jelly donut filled with mustard. The variation below looks a little different from the store-bought kind, but it's easier to make.

Jelly Donuts (Berliners)

Pfannkuchen

2 cups + 3 tablespoons flour
1 yeast cake (2¼ tablespoons)
¼ cup sugar
1 cup lukewarm milk
8 tablespoons butter, at room temperature
salt
grated lemon peel (from ½ unprocessed lemon)
3 egg yolks

For the work surface: **flour**

For the filling:
**jelly or jam or your choice (apricot, cherry, raspberry, etc.)
oil for deep frying
powdered sugar for dusting, or sugar for dredging**

1 For the dough, sift the flour into a bowl and make a depression in the middle. Crumble yeast cake into the depression, add sugar and milk. Dust with a little flour from the edge; chop butter and distribute around the edge. Cover the bowl and set aside to rise in a warm, draft-free place, about 30 minutes.

2 Knead the dough with the salt, lemon peel, and egg yolks. Cover again and let stand 1 hour.

3 Knead the dough well on a floured work surface and flatten (or roll out). On half the dough, punch out circles with a glass or cup. Put a teaspoon of jam or jelly in the middle of each circle.

4 On the remaining half of the dough, use the glass or cup to surround and cut or punch out more circles of dough; place these over the tops of the first circles (the ones with the jelly), and the edges together, to seal.

5 Turn the donuts over on a floured work surface and cover with a cloth; let sit about 30 minutes. They should rise noticeably.

6 Heat the oil to a boil (360 degrees). Place the donuts in the oil, a few at a time, and fry until golden brown and crispy on both sides.

7 Let the oil drain off the donuts through a sieve. Dust immediately with sugar or powdered sugar.

Tip: These taste great with a rum glaze—stir together ¾ cup powdered sugar with 1 or 2 tablespoons of rum until smooth; spread over the top of each donut.

Variation:
Cameroons

Kameruner

One variation on this recipe is the cameroon. Pfannkuchen/jelly donuts are more common on café menus in the West, and cameroons are more common on café menus in the East.

Roll out the yeast dough in the recipe above and divide into 12 portions. Knead each portion once more and form into the shape of a bone or log. Cover and let rise 30 minutes. Deep-fry in hot oil, remove, and roll in sugar.

Tip: Cameroons are only found in Berlin. The name probably dates back to imperial times, as Cameroon was a German colony in Africa from 1884 to 1916.

"Shoe-Sole" Pastries

Blätterteiggebäck "Schuhsohlen"

"*Sweet-toothed Berliners*" *love their coffee substitute with danishes—and lots of cream.*

Makes 4 servings:

8 ounces frozen pastry dough, thawed
¼ cup course sugar
1½ cups cream
2 pkgs. vanilla sugar*
   (3½ teaspoons), or 2 teaspoons vanilla extract

Other:
baking parchment

Garnish with:
Sugar or powdered sugar

1 Preheat oven to 390 degrees. Cut the pastry dough into circles about 2¾ inches in diameter.

2 Place each circle of dough on some coarse sugar and flatten to the size and shape of a shoe sole or tongue.

3 Place the dough shapes on a baking pan lined with baking parchment, and put the pan on the middle rack of the preheated oven. Bake for 10 minutes, until golden brown and crispy.

4 Place the crispy dough shapes on a work surface. Beat the cream with the vanilla sugar until it forms peaks; use an icing bag to carefully squirt cream onto half of the shoe soles.

5 Place the rest of the shoe soles on top, and dust with sugar or powdered sugar.

*If commercial vanilla sugar is not available, make your own: slice open one vanilla bean and scrape contents into 2 cups sugar in an airtight container. You can use a fresh bean or one used in a previous recipe (e.g., a custard—let stand several hours if the bean is damp when combined with the sugar). You can substitute 1 teaspoon vanilla extract for 1 pkg. vanilla sugar, but this works better in batters and doughs than in toppings.

Love Bones

Liebesknochen

Even this sweet dish is an example of Huguenot influence, because they were the ones who brought éclairs from France. In Berlin, however, French éclairs were renamed "Liebesknochen" (love bones).

For the pastry:
½ cup milk
½ cup water
1 tablespoon sugar
salt
8 tablespoons butter
½ cup flour
4 eggs

For the filling:
1 cup milk
1 pkg. vanilla sugar (1¾ teaspoons), or 1 teaspoon vanilla extract
3 egg yolks
½ cup sugar
1 tablespoon flour
2 tablespoons freeze-dried, instant coffee
2 egg whites

For the glaze:
1 cup powdered sugar
2 tablespoons cocoa powder
1 tablespoon melted butter

For the baking pan:
baking parchment

1. For the pastry, bring milk, water, sugar, salt, and butter to a brief boil. Remove the pot from the stove and stir in the flour, all at once.

2. Place the pot back on the burner and beat the dough with a wooden spoon until the dough forms a ball and lifts from the bottom of the pot. Remove the pot from the stove and stir in 1 egg. Once the first egg is completely mixed in, stir in the next egg, and so on, until all 4 eggs are mixed in.

3. Preheat the oven to 390 degrees, and line the baking pan with baking parchment. Put the dough into an icing bag—with jagged spout—a little at a time, and squirt 12 strips, each about 4 inches long, onto the pan.

4. Place the baking pan on the middle rack in the preheated oven and bake the dough strips about 30 minutes, until golden

brown. Remove the pastries from the oven and cool on a wire rack.

5 In the meantime, bring the milk and vanilla sugar (or vanilla extract) to a boil and remove the pot from the stove. Using an electric hand mixer, beat the egg yolks and sugar in a heat-proof bowl, until creamy. Add the flour and instant coffee.

6 Add the milk, a little at a time, placing the bowl in a hot water bath (double boiler). The cream should be airy and thick. Beat the egg whites until stiff and stir into the cream; chill briefly.

7 Cut the pastries lengthwise, along the side, but do not cut all the way through. Put the cream in an icing bag and squirt into the opening in the dough. For the glaze, stir the powdered sugar, cocoa, and butter together in a pot and heat until hot and creamy. Brush onto the love bones. As soon as they've dried, eat them!

Bee Stings

Bienenstich

1 pound flour
1 fresh yeast cake
    (2¼ tablespoons)
½ cup sugar
1 cup lukewarm milk
8 tablespoons butter, room
    temperature
2 eggs
salt

For the topping:
12 tablespoons butter
⅔ cup sugar
1 pkg. vanilla sugar
    (1¾ teaspoons)
½ cup sliced almonds
5 tablespoons milk

For the filling:
2 cups milk
1 pkg. vanilla pudding powder
salt
¼ cup sugar
12 tablespoons melted butter

Other:
flour for the work surface
baking parchment for the
    baking tray

1 Sift the flour into a bowl and make a depression in the middle. Crumble yeast cake into the depression, sprinkle sugar, pour in milk, and dust with flour from the edge. Cover and place in a warm, draft-free place for 20 minutes.

2 Knead butter, eggs, and salt into the dough, cover again, and let stand another 20 minutes.

3 Turn the dough onto a floured work surface and knead well; roll out to the thickness of a finger. Preheat oven to 390 degrees, and line a baking pan with baking parchment.

4 Place the dough on the pan and poke several times with a fork. Let rise another 10 minutes.

5 In the meantime, heat the butter, sugar, and vanilla sugar in a pot, stirring constantly. Stir in the sliced almonds and milk.

6 Remove the pot from the stove. Once the contents have cooled, spread over the surface of the dough.

7 Place the baking pan on the middle rack in the preheated oven and bake for about 30 minutes. Remove from the oven, allow to cool briefly, and cut the cake into small rectangles.

8 To make the filling, stir four teaspoons milk with the pudding powder until smooth. Add a dash of salt and sugar to the rest of the milk and heat; stir in the pudding/milk mixture. Heat to a boil and remove from the stove.

9 Add the butter to the pudding, stirring vigorously. Cut each piece of cake horizontally through the middle, remove the tops, spread the bottoms with pudding, and replace the tops.

Crumb Cake and Coffee with Chickory

Streuselkuchen und Muckefuck

Today, "Muckefuck" means coffee from chickory, but originally, that was the general term for the new drink from America, that took some getting used to, since simpler folks who weren't royalty couldn't afford it. And Berliners love crumb cake above all else—though the original recipe came from Silesia, a principality southeast of Berlin what is now Poland. "Streusel" (crumble topping) goes well not just with coffee, but with a "Dicke" too: sour milk (buttermilk) with a thick layer of grated dark bread, sugar, and cinnamon.

For the cake:
4 cups flour
½ fresh yeast cake (approx. 1⅛ tablespoons)
¼ cup sugar
1 cup lukewarm milk
6 tablespoons butter, at room temperature
salt

For the crumb topping:
1 cup flour
1 cup sugar
½ teaspoon ground cinnamon
12 tablespoons cold butter, cut into pieces

Other:
flour for the work surface

For the baking pan:
baking parchment

Serve with:
1 cup whipped cream

1 To make the dough, sift the flour into a bowl and make a depression in the middle. Crumble the yeast into the depression, sprinkle with sugar, and pour in milk.

2 Dust with flour from the edges; chop butter and distribute around the edge. Cover the bowl and let the dough rise in a warm, draft-free place, about 30 minutes.

3 Knead the dough with the salt until smooth, cover with a towel, and let rise 30 minutes. Line the baking pan with baking parchment. Knead the dough

on a floured surface, flatten, spreading to the size of the baking pan, and place the dough on the paper-lined pan. Press the edges up and let rise another 30 minutes.

4 Preheat the oven to 390 degrees. On a work surface, knead the flour, sugar, cinnamon, and butter pieces together and crumble into a streusel over the surface of the dough.

5 Place the baking pan on the middle rack of the preheated oven, and bake the crumb cake until golden in color, about 30 minutes. Remove from the oven, let cool briefly, and cut into serving pieces. Serve with thick whipped cream.

Tip: For a more elegant "Sunday Streusel," add ¼ cup chopped almonds.

Marzipan–Rhubarb Crumb Cake

Marzipankuchen mit Rhabarber und Streuseln

Ingredients for one 12-inch springform cake pan

For the butter-crumb streusel—Berliners love lots of streusel!
- ⅔ cups flour
- ½ cup sugar
- 1 pkg. vanilla sugar (1¾ teaspoons)
- 1 pinch salt
- 5.5 oz. butter, cut in slivers, room temperature

For the batter:
- 5.5 oz. softened butter
- 5.5 oz. marzipan paste
- 1 pkg. vanilla sugar (1¾ teaspoons)
- 4 eggs (medium)
- 1 cup flour
- 2 teaspoons of baking powder
- ½ cup milk

For the filling:
- 2 pounds rhubarb, washed and cut in ½-inch pieces
- ½ cup sugar
- 5.5 oz. crème fraîche*

1 For the streusel, combine flour, sugar, vanilla sugar, and a pinch of salt with the butter, using an electric hand-mixer with a dough hook. Crumble the streusel by hand.

2 Boil the rhubarb 10–15 minutes with ½ cup sugar in some water. Let cool.

3 For the batter, stir the butter, eggs, marzipan (crumbled into small pieces), and vanilla sugar until creamy. Stir in the flour, baking powder, and milk, a little at a time.

---

*To make your own crème fraîche, mix 2 tablespoons buttermilk with 1 cup whipping cream in a glass container. Cover. Let stand at room temperature for 8–24 hours, or until thick. Keeps (refrigerated) up to 10 days.

4 Pour the batter in a greased pan. Spread the rhubarb over the batter and spoon crème fraîche over the fruit. Sprinkle the streusel on top and bake about one hour in a preheated 350-degree oven.

Tip: You can skip boiling the rhubarb and simply stir it into the batter with the crème fraîche.

Apple Crumb Cake

Apfelstreuselkuchen

This is a simpler variation of the rhubarb cake, but more common in Berlin.

For the butter-crumb streusel:
⅔ cups flour
½ cup sugar
1 pkg. or 2 teaspoons of vanilla sugar
1 pinch salt
5 oz. butter, cut in slivers, room temperature

For the batter:
5.5 oz. softened butter
1 pkg. or 2 teaspoons of vanilla sugar
2 eggs (medium)
1 cup flour
2 teaspoons of baking powder

For the filling:
1.5 pounds of apples, cut in ½-inch pieces

1. For the streusel, combine flour, sugar, vanilla sugar, and salt with the butter, using an electric hand-mixer with a dough hook. Crumble the streusel by hand.

2. For the batter, stir the butter, eggs, and vanilla sugar until creamy. Stir in the flour together with the baking powder, a little at a time.

3. Pour the batter in a greased pan. Peel the apples and cut them to thin slices. Spread them over the batter. Sprinkle the streusel on top and bake about one half hour in a preheated 350-degree oven until the streusels are brown.

Tip: You can add some chopped walnuts to the apples.

Red Fruit Pudding with Werder Fruits

Rote Grütze mit Früchten aus Werder

The Werder region lies to the south and west, by the gates of Berlin, right under Potsdam, and is a veritable oasis of fruits and vegetables. Every year, there's a tree-blossom celebration in Werder—and they have everything: tart cherries, strawberries, raspberries, red currants, plums, pears, apples, and sweet cherries, in fruit form, and as wine, by the glass, or in bottles to take home. What better way for Berliners to have their own personal Werder-blossom celebration, than with red fruit pudding and plenty of cream?

Makes 6 to 8 servings:

2 pounds fresh red berries and pitted cherries (raspberries, currants, sweet and sour cherries)
½ cup sugar
3 tablespoons cornstarch
1 cup cream

1. Wash the berries and place them in a wide pot. Sprinkle with ½ cup sugar, pour in 2 cups water, and bring to a boil. Reduce the heat, and stir a ladleful of the water with the cornstarch, until smooth.

2. Return to the pot, stirring, until thickened. Pour the contents of the pot into a serving bowl. Sprinkle a little sugar over the top and chill cool.

Tip: Serve with cream.

"Berlin Air" with Red Berries

"Berliner Luft" mit roten Beeren

"Berliner Luft" (Berlin air) is a dessert with an airy egg cream, reminiscent of an 1904 song by Paul Lincke, which quickly became a hit and is still sung today: "Das ist die Berliner Luft, Luft, Luft…" (That's the Berlin air, air, air…)

Makes 4 servings:

- 4 eggs
- 1 cup sugar
- 3 teaspoons cornstarch
- 5 ounces (⅝ cup) apple juice
- juice from 1 lemon
- 1 cup whipping cream
- 1 pkg. vanilla sugar (1¾ teaspoons), or 1 teaspoon vanilla extract
- 1 pound mixed berries (strawberries, raspberries, red currants)

1. In a heat-proof bowl, stir together the eggs, a heaping ½ cup sugar, cornstarch, apple juice, and lemon juice, place over a hot water bath (double boiler), and whip until creamy and airy.

2. Remove the bowl from the pot, and beat the cream again. Beat the whipping cream and vanilla sugar (or vanilla extract) until stiff, and mix with the cream in the bowl. Cover and chill in the refrigerator for about 2 hours.

3. In the meantime, wash the berries, cut the strawberries into smaller pieces, and put all of the berries into a pot with the rest of the sugar and ½ cup water; heat for several minutes; cool briefly. Serve the cream in individual bowls, spooning the berries on top.

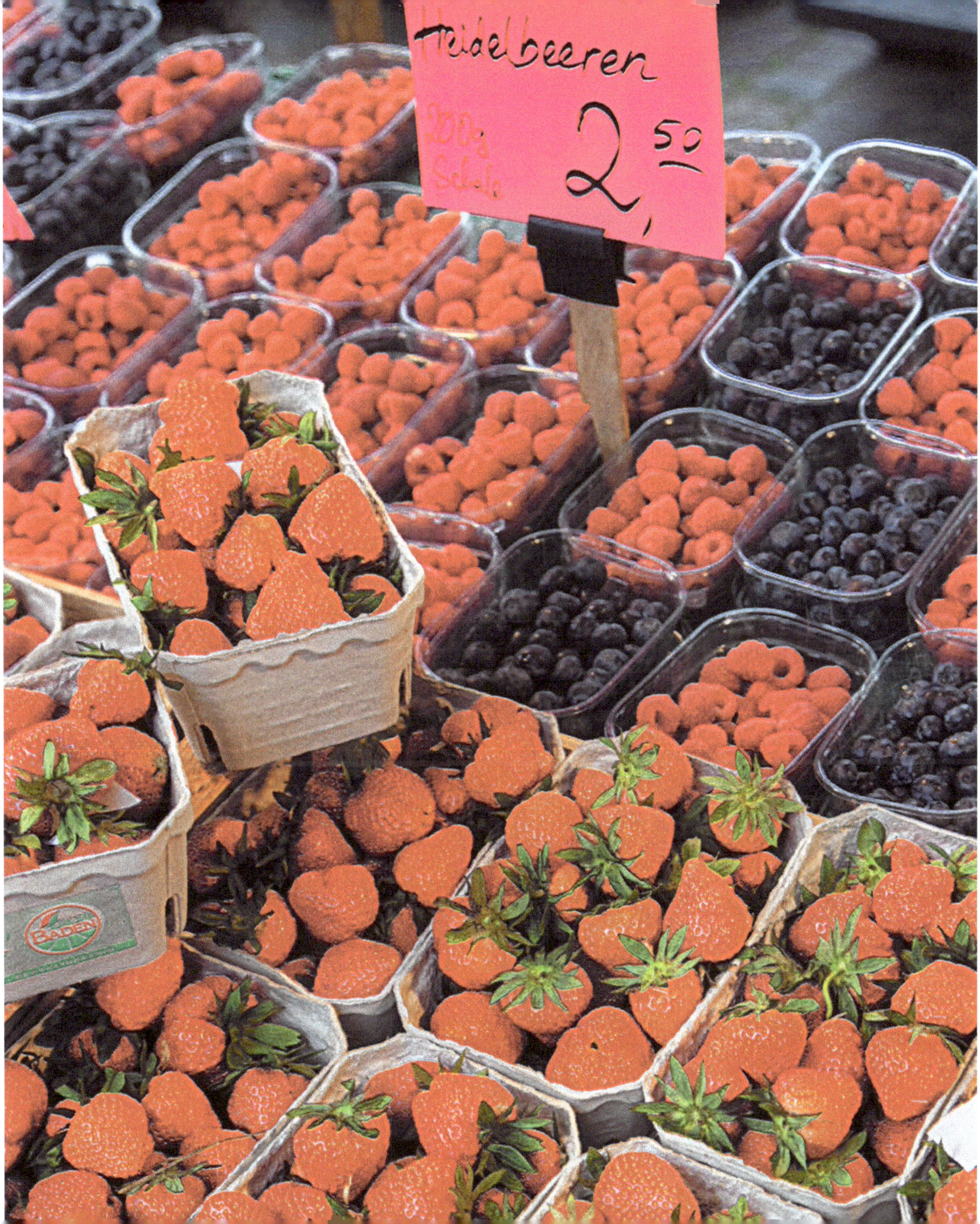

Heidelbeeren
200g Schale
2,50
BADEN

Index

apple crumb bake, 90
Aunt Hannelore's lentil stew, 61
bacon-and-egg sandwiches, open-faced, 23
bee stings, 84
beef roulades, 53
Berlin air with red berries, 92
Berlin broth potatoes, 68
Berliners (Jelly Donuts), 79
Berliner liver, pan-fried, 48
Berliner Weisse, 8
Bismarckherring, 24
Bockwurst with potato salad, 16
braised cucumbers, 77
bratwurst, 50
bread, 14
cabbage leaves, stuffed, Grandpa Lothar, 63
cameroons, 80
carp, Polish-style, 33
chicken fricassee, not-so-elegant, 64
crayfish tails in dill sauce, 34
crumb cake and coffee with chicory, 88
crumb cake, marzipan-rhubarb, 88
cucumbers, braised, 77
cutlets in aspic, 22
Currywurst with fries, 19
donuts, jelly (Berliner), 79
döner kebab, 20
Dönnhoffplatz, roast goose, 54
eel, green, 28
eel, old-Berlin-style, 29
eggs with mustard sauce, 72
eggs, pickled, 12

Emperor Wilhelm II's potato soup, 60
fat, crackling, on sliced bread, 14
faux rabbit meatloaf, 46
filleted pickled herring, 24
fried tench in dill butter, 36
goose dripping on rye rolls, 14
goose, roasted, Dönhoffplatz, 54
Grandpa Lothar's stuffed cabbage leaves, 63
green eel, 28
"Hackepeter" (minced steak), 15
hash, leftover, 67
Havel River zander with braised cucumbers, 30
herring, filleted and pickled, 24
herring, fried and pickled, 27
herring sauce, 24
Holstein-style schnitzel, 38
home fried potatoes, 70
kale, 74
Königsberg meatballs, 47
leftover hash, 57
lentil stew, 61
liver, Berliner, pan-fried, 49
love bones, 82
marzipan-rhubarb crumb cake, 88
mashed potatoes, 66
meatballs, 10
meatballs, Königsberg, 47
meatloaf, faux rabbit, 46
meatloaf, seasoned and raw, on rolls, 15
minced steak (Hackepeter), 15
Mother Gerlinde's beef roulades, 53
noodles, thick, with eggs and bureaucrat's sauce, 56
not-so-elegant chicken fricassee, 64

old-Berlin-style eel, 29
pan-fried Berliner liver, 49
pea soup with ears and snouts, 59
Perch in beer sauce, 36
Polish-style carp, 33
pork knuckle with broth, 42
pork loin, smoked, with sauerkraut, 41
potatoes, Berlin broth, 68
potatoes, mashed, 66
potatoe pancakes, 69
potato purée, 68
potato salad with Bockwurst, 17
potato soup, "Emperor Wilhelm II", 60
proud Henry's thick bratwurst, 50
puréed peas, 73
red fruit Pudding with Werder berries, 91
rollmops, 26
rutabaga stew, 58
sandwiches, ham and egg, open-faced, 23
sauerkraut, with smoked pork loin, 41
schnitzel à la Holstein, 38
"shoe-sole" pastries, 81
smoked pork loin with sauerkraut, 41
Teltow turnips, 74
tench, fried, in dill butter, 36
thick egg noodles with bureaucrat's sauce, 56
turnips, Teltow, 74
veal cakes, 45
zander, Havel River, with braised cucumbers, 30

Thanks

Berlinica would like to thank the KaDeWe, Berlin's biggest department store, located at Wittenbergplatz, for the gracious picture permit. The photos on pages 11, 25, 26, 29, 31, 32, 35, 69, 71, 82, and 83, were taken at the KaDeWe food department. Most of the outdoor pictures are from Winterfeldt Market, Berlin.

Rose Marie Donhauser

is an experienced cook, cookbook author, travel journalist, food critic, and a member of the jury of Berlin's master chefs, which annually honors the city's best restaurants.

Berlinica presents

2010–2015 Program

Welcome to Berlinica, the first American publishing company devoted to Berlin! If you subscribe to our monthly newsletter at

www.berlinica.com/contact.html

You will get one of those two e-books below for free. All you need to do is go to our website and sign up.

New Berlinica books in 2015

Erik Kirschbaum
Burning Beethoven
The Eradication of German Culture in the United States in World War I
Preface by Herb Stupp

Softcover, 176 pp., 20 pictures, $14.95, ISBN: 978-1-935902-85-0

"Powerful retelling of a forgotten piece of American history"

Kurt Tucholsky
Prayer After the Slaughter
Poems from World War I
Bilingual Edition, translated by Peter Appelbaum and James Scott

Softcover, 116 pp., 6 bw pictures, $12.95, ISBN: 978-1-935902-28-7

"He heaped scorn on the reactionary institutions of the old regime"

Sebastian Ringel
Leipzig!
One Thousand Years of German History
Bach, Luther, Faust: The City of Books and Music

Softcover, 224 pp., color, $25.95 ISBN: 978-1-935902-58-1

"Humerous and tragic stories from 1000 years of Leipzig"

Michael Brettin/Peter Kroh
Berlin 1945
World War II: Photos of the Aftermath
From the Soviet Army Archives
With a Preface by Steven Kinzer

Softcover, 218 pp., 177 bw photos $25.95, ISBN: 978-1-935902-02-7

"Even if you think you've seen it all, Berlin 1945 will surprise you"

Erik Kirschbaum
ROCKING THE WALL
BRUCE SPRINGSTEEN: THE BERLIN CONCERT THAT CHANGED THE WORLD

Softcover, 168 pp., 45 color pictures, $16.95, ISBN: 978-1-935902-82-9

"A statement of the power of music as anyone, ever, has come up with"

Kurt Tucholsky
RHEINSBERG
A Storybook for Lovers
Hardcover, 96 pp., $14.95
ISBN: 978-1-935902-25-6

Kurt Tucholsky
BERLIN! BERLIN!
DISPATCHES FROM THE WEIMAR REPUBLIC

Preface by Anne Nelson
Introduction by Ian King

Softcover, 198 pp., 41 pictures, $13.95
ISBN: 978-1-935902-23-2

". . . the most brilliant, prolific, and witty cultural journalist of his time"

Andreas Austilat
MARK TWAIN IN BERLIN
NEWLY DISCOVERED STORIES & AN ACCOUNT OF TWAIN'S BERLIN ADVENTURES
Preface by Lewis Lapham

Softcover, 176 pp., 67 bw pictures, $13.95, ISBN: 978-1-935902-95-9

"This fascinating book is a must-read for any Twain enthusiast"

Holly-Jane Rahlens
WALLFLOWER
A Novel
Softcover, 150 pp., $11.95
ISBN: 978-1-935902-70-6

City History and Present

remnants, ruins, remembrances
The Berlin Wall Today
with a preface by
Michael Cramer
photos Eva C. Schweitzer
Berlinica

Rose Marie Donhauser

The Berlin Cookbook

Traditional Recipes and Nourishing Stories

Hardcover, 104 pp., $21.95
61 recipes, 98 color pictures
ISBN: 978-1-935902-51-5

"Beautiful pictures, entertaining texts, and easy to process, fresh ingredients"

Berlin for Free
A Guidebook to Music, Movies, Museums
and More for the Frugal Traveler
Originally Published by Verlag an der Spree
Berlinica

Monika Maertens

Berlin for Free

A Guidebook to Movies, Museums, Music, and More for the Frugal Traveler

Softcover, 104 pp., $11.95
ISBN: 978-1-935902-40-9

"This book is an investment that pays for itself—whoever wants, or has to save, needs it"

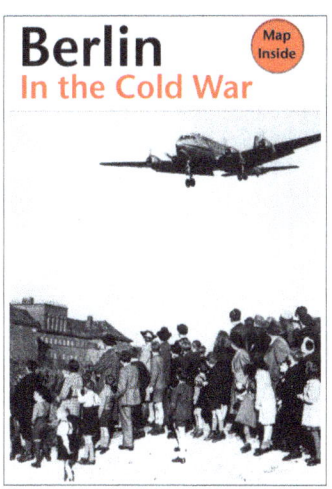

Andreas Nachama, Julius H. Schoeps,
and Hermann Simon
Jews
in Berlin
Berlinica
Updated Edition

Andreas Nachama
Julius Schoeps
Hermann Simon

Jews in Berlin

Preface by Carol Kahn-Strauss

Softcover, 314 pp., $25.95
376 pictures, color & b/w
ISBN: 978-1-935902-60-7

". . . a captivating read that promises a wealth of enjoyment . . ."

Berlin
In the Cold War
Map Inside

Thomas Flemming

Berlin in the Cold War – The Battle for the Divided City

Softcover, 90 pp., $11.95
51 bw pictures, 3 maps
ISBN: 978-1-935902-80-5

"The story of the divided city in a nutshell, without missing a beat"

DVDs, CDs, and Angels

Adrienne Haan
Berlin — mon amour
A tribute to 1920s Germany in music

Music CD, 50 minutes
In English or German
$ 15.95, only on Amazon

"Grace, elegance, power"

Rosemarie Reed
The Path to Nuclear Fission
Narrated by Linda Hunt

Movie DVD, run time 81 min
German / English, subtitled
$19.95, only on Amazon

"... honors the lives of women who were more than significant ..."

Stefan Roloff
The Red Orchestra
A documentary about the German anti-Nazi Resistance

Movie DVD, run time 57 min.
German and English, subtitled
$24.95, only on Amazon

". . . danger invaded normalcy . . . landscape threatens to tumble . . ."

Lothar Heinke
Wings of Desire Angels of Berlin

Softcover, 102 pp., $19.95
123 full color pictures
ISBN: 978-1-935902-18-8

"A book full of anecdotes about the angels throughout the city — and a search for angelic traces"

www.ingramcontent.com/pod-product-compliance
Lightning Source LLC
Chambersburg PA
CBHW061128070526
44584CB00033B/4250
9781935902508